EUGÈNE DELACROIX'S THEORY OF ART

PRINCETON MONOGRAPH

IN ART AND ARCHAEOLOGY

XXXVII

PUBLISHED FOR THE

DEPARTMENT OF ART AND ARCHAEOLOGY

PRINCETON UNIVERSITY

EUGÈNE DELACROIX'S THEORY OF ART

BY GEORGE P. MRAS

PRINCETON, NEW JERSEY

PRINCETON UNIVERSITY PRESS

1966

TO MY MOTHER

PREFACE

THE LITERARY ENDEAVORS of Eugène Delacroix, especially the
Journal, have long been ranked among the most significant
nonvisual contributions by a major artist to the history of art. Rich
in anecdote, criticism, philosophy, and biography, and expressed
in a persuasive prose style, these writings have inspired widespread
admiration. For the student of art theory they possess special value
in that few artists have revealed the inner core of a basic aesthetic
in so thorough a manner. The industrious reader of the Journal,
along with a formidable mass of articles and letters, inevitably approaches the vast corpus of his paintings armed with profound insights into the aim and method of his art. This reader also goes
armed with an extraordinarily comprehensive and complex mixture of traditional and original theory. For Delacroix, like his
illustrious predecessor, Leonardo da Vinci, used past theory as
fundamental raw material in the structure of his thought. Therefore, it is incorrect to suggest, in the words of one writer, that his
"philosophie de l'art est, essentiellement, la philosophie de *son* art
et de *son* génie."[1] A systematic investigation of his thought reveals
that Delacroix was dependent to a surprising degree upon antecedent theory for his ideas. The revolutionary aspects of his dynamic, romantic art rested on a solid foundation of knowledge of
traditional art theory.

This study of Delacroix's aesthetic aims to identify the major
sources of his theory, to isolate the derived elements of his thought
from original contributions, and to relate his theory to his art. In
addition, the very pattern of his selection of ideas from the past
offers further insight into the nature of his romanticism.

Since Delacroix's acquaintance with traditional theory was of
wide range, it seemed best to place certain limitations upon the
scope of this study. In order to maintain focus on its principal sub-

[1] Hubert Gillot, *E. Delacroix: l'homme, ses idées, son œuvre*, Paris, 1928, p. ii.

ject — his selection, adaptation and use of past theory — I have made no attempt to furnish complete histories of the manifold topics treated by the artist. In general (major exceptions are the writings of the Abbé Dubos and André Félibien), the background material is limited to authorities known by Delacroix, although in two cases (the sections dealing with the sketch and the *paragone*) the subjects seemed of sufficient interest to encourage violation of this rule. Also, for the same purpose, I have not attempted to exhaust all of his theoretical statements or the minor influences on his thought.

This journey of exploration into the vast and subtle seas of art theory would have been impossible without the aid and encouragement of my colleagues. Professor Rensselaer W. Lee first suggested the topic and has unstintingly provided valuable advice and criticism during the genesis of this work. Professor Robert Rosenblum generously volunteered to read the text and has rendered numerous suggestions for its improvement. To Professor Donald D. Egbert I am indebted for aid in shaping the material into a viable format. During his years at Princeton, Professor William Seitz of Brandeis University shed steady light on the significance of Delacroix's art and ideas. Professor H. W. Janson of New York University was especially helpful in providing pertinent criticism of my discussion of Delacroix's *paragone*. And for the opportunity to begin this study under ideal conditions I am grateful for the aid provided by Princeton University in the form of a Procter and Gamble Faculty Fellowship granted in the Fall of 1961.

For permission to quote extensively from the French edition of Delacroix's Journal, I am indebted to Crown Publishers (*The Journal of Eugène Delacroix*, ed. André Joubin. Translated from the French by Walter Pach. © 1948 by Crown Publishers, Inc. Used by permission of Crown Publishers, Inc.). Librarie Plon (*Correspondance générale d'Eugène Delacroix*, ed. André Joubin), Editions Garnier Frères (*Curiosités esthétiques, L'Art romantique et autres œuvres critiques de Baudelaire*, ed. Henri Lemaitre), E. P. Dutton and Co., Inc. (Joseph Addison and Richard Steele, *The Spectator*, ed. G. Gregory Smith, Everyman's Library), and Henry E. Huntington Library and Art Gallery (*Sir Joshua Reynolds: Discourses on Art*, ed. Robert R. Wark) also granted permission to quote from

PREFACE

their publications. And Professor Bates Lowry, editor of *The Art Bulletin*, graciously allowed me to incorporate into the text my two articles, "Literary Sources of Delacroix's Conception of the Sketch and the Imagination," and *"Ut Pictura Musica*: A Study of Delacroix's *Paragone."*

Princeton, N.J.
February 28, 1966   G E O R G E P. M R A S

ACKNOWLEDGMENTS

ALL ILLUSTRATIONS appearing in this volume are from the *Archives photographiques* with the exception of the following:

3. Photo Bulloz

8. Ulrich Christoffel, *Eugène Delacroix*

10. Bernheim-Jeune et Cie., Paris

12. Raymond Escholier, *Delacroix: peintre, graveur, écrivain*

21. Chicago Art Institute

22. Alte Pinakothek, Munich

24. Reinhart Collection, Winterthur

30. A. Noyer

32. Museum of Fine Arts, Boston

35. Metropolitan Museum of Art, New York
(Permission of V. W. Van Gogh, Laren, Holland)

CONTENTS

LIST OF ILLUSTRATIONS

Unless otherwise indicated, the work is by Delacroix.

1. *Orpheus Bringing Civilization to the Primitive Greeks,* 1843-47, oil and wax on plaster, Library, Palais Bourbon, Paris
2. *Attila and His Hordes Overrun Italy and the Arts,* 1843-47, oil and wax on plaster, Library, Palais Bourbon, Paris
3. Gustave Courbet, *Bathers,* 1853, oil on canvas, Fabre Museum, Montpellier
4. *Jacob Wrestling with the Angel,* 1854-61, oil and wax on plaster, Chapel of the Holy Angels, Church of Saint-Sulpice, Paris
5. *Dante and Virgil,* 1822, oil on canvas, Louvre, Paris
6. *Death of Sardanapalus,* 1827, oil on canvas, Louvre, Paris
7. *Massacre at Chios,* 1824, oil on canvas, Louvre, Paris
8. *Heliodorus Driven from the Temple,* 1854-61, oil and wax on plaster, Chapel of the Holy Angels, Church of Saint-Sulpice, Paris
9. *Lion Mauling a Dead Arab,* 1847, oil on canvas, National Gallery, Oslo
10. *Indian Woman Gnawed by a Tiger,* 1852, oil on canvas, Private Collection
11. *Seated Nude: Mademoiselle Rose,* 1821-23, oil on canvas, Louvre, Paris
12. Study of a detail for the decoration of the Salon of Peace, Hôtel de Ville, Paris (destroyed by fire, 1871), 1852-54, pencil, Louvre, Paris
13. *Study of an Algerian Interior,* 1832, water color and pencil, Louvre, Paris
14. *Studies of Arab Women,* 1832, water color and pencil, Louvre, Paris
15. *Algerian Women in Their Apartment,* 1834, oil on canvas, Louvre, Paris

LIST OF ILLUSTRATIONS

EUGÈNE DELACROIX'S THEORY OF ART

INTRODUCTION

To ANYONE REQUIRED to compile a list of the salient characteristics of Romanticism it becomes immediately apparent that the catalogue — which would certainly include feverish activity of the imagination, extreme subjectivity, exploitation of the emotions, predilection for revolt, and longing for the unknown and the unattainable — might also serve as a psychological portrait of youth. These Romantic qualities naturally flourish in the restless, unsettled world of the young. And, as years and experience accumulate, they usually subside — if only because a sustained commitment to such a program would place a formidable strain on the physical and mental resources of the aging adult. By 1850, Romanticism itself had for some time suffered the chastening effects of middle age. The battles, enthusiasms, and excesses of the early years lived now only in memory. In France, the old revolutionaries in painting were confronted in turn with the revolt of Courbet, who brazenly denied the efficacy of the Romantic imagination in his supremely factual offerings of that year — *Burial at Ornans* and *Stone Breakers*. The time had come, perhaps, when the audacious experiment called Romanticism could be viewed with some detachment. Having ventured to the brink of the mysterious wellsprings of human irrationality and having relished the enthralling experience, the middle-aged European could now sit back and wonder at the temerity of the venture. He might ponder the implications of August Wilhelm von Schlegel's invocation of dark and dangerous powers when he defined Romantic poetry as "the expression of the secret attraction to a chaos which lies concealed in the very bosom of the ordered universe, and is perpetually striving after new and marvellous births. . . ."[1]

Eugène Delacroix, perhaps more than any other French artist,

[1] August Wilhelm von Schlegel, *Lectures on Dramatic Art and Literature*, tr. John Black, 2d ed., London, 1894, p. 343.

had felt this "secret attraction" to chaos and had forged a free and revolutionary technique in order to render it visible. Being French, however, he sensed the danger of his commitment and on May 1, 1850, in the fastness of his country retreat at Champrosay, recorded in his Journal rather pessimistic and unfavorable thoughts on the Romantic flirtation with the uncivilized. Apropos of Jean-Jacques Rousseau's sanctification of the savage he queried: "Mais l'homme lui-même, quand il s'abandonne à l'instinct sauvage qui est le fond même de sa nature, ne conspire-t-il pas avec les éléments pour détruire les beaux ouvrages? La barbarie ne vient-elle presque périodiquement, et semblable à la Furie qui attend Sisyphe roulant sa pierre au haut de la montagne pour renverser et confondre, pour faire la nuit après une trop vive lumière? Et ce je ne sais quoi qui a donné à l'homme une intelligence supérieure à celle des bêtes, ne semble-t-il pas prendre plaisir à le punir de cette intelligence même?"[2]

No one was better equipped to challenge Rousseau for no one had come closer to empathy with savagery. No one had understood or rendered so well the combined grace, physical power, and irrationality of wild beasts. And no one had been more alert to the seductive beauty of this combination. Yet, and this contributes to his position as one of the crucial personalities of the nineteenth century, few artists were so profoundly knowledgeable of the traditions of European culture. Readers of the Journal of this most farouche of painters encounter myriad references to the most surprising sources. Horace, Boileau, Montesquieu, and Voltaire are cited frequently; and words of praise for such non-Romantic artists as Poussin, Lebrun, Racine, and Cimarosa abound.

For those critics who have described Classicism and Romanticism as separate and fiercely opposed entities this enthusiasm for the

[2] André Joubin (ed.), *Journal d'Eugène Delacroix*, Paris, 1960, I, p. 360. The attitude expressed in this passage had already been vividly dramatized in visual terms in his monumental decorations for the library of the Palais Bourbon (1843-47) where the benefits of civilization are opposed to the savagery and destructive force of barbarism. In an elaborate iconographical scheme, the products of civilization (science, philosophy, law, theology, and poetry) shine forth in a series of five cupolas while in hemicycles at opposite ends of the room, one sees Orpheus as the purveyor of the arts of peace to mankind (Fig. 1) and Attila as the destroyer of Italian civilization (Fig. 2). See Maurice Sérullaz, *Les peintures murales de Delacroix*, Paris, 1963, pp. 49-77

achievements in art and theory of members of the Classical persuasion has been regarded as suspect — as manifestation of a reprehensible apostasy from the true, revolutionary cause. No comfort, moreover, could be found in his oft-stated aversion to any direct affiliation with Romantic coteries. "Les écoles, les coteries," he wrote (with specific reference to Romantic groups), "ne sont autre chose que des associations de médiocrités, pour se garantir mutuellement un semblant de renommée qui à la vérité est de courte durée mais qui fait traverser la vie agréablement."[3] No comfort either in a story which dramatizes his sensitivity on this score. When an admirer, whom he encountered at the Luxembourg Palace, declared, "Monsieur Delacroix, vous êtes le Victor Hugo de la peinture," Delacroix coldly responded, "Je suis un pur classique."[4]

Not surprisingly, a number of widely divergent theories have risen concerning the nature of Delacroix's Romanticism — a problem of vital importance for all French painting of the first half of the nineteenth century. Generally, critics have been divided into two camps: those who consider Delacroix an outright Romantic in his art despite the Classical ideas and preferences that emerge in his writings, and those who favor some synthesis of his Romantic and Classical tendencies.

Already in the mid-nineteenth century Théophile Gautier raised the issue of an apparent dichotomy between the artist's theory and his practice, maintaining that "jamais œuvre ne ressembla moins à l'idéal de l'artiste qui l'exécuta que celui d'Eugène Delacroix. On aurait pu croire que c'était chez lui un jeu d'esprit d'avancer des théories contraires à sa pratique, mais tout nous fait croire qu'il était sincère en émettant ces idées, si étranges dans sa bouche. Seulement, quand il était devant sa toile, sa palette au pouce, au milieu d'un atelier où ne pénétrait personne et où régnait une température de serre pour les plantes tropicales, il oubliait ses classiques opinions de la veille. . . ."[5] And in 1869 Delacroix's

[3] From a letter to his friend Madame Cavé, dated Friday, June 8, 1855, by André Joubin (ed.), *Correspondance générale d'Eugène Delacroix*, Paris, 1936-38, III, p. 265.
[4] See Paul Jamot, "Delacroix," *Le romantisme et l'art*, preface by E. Herriot, Paris, 1928, p. 101.
[5] Théophile Gautier, *Histoire du romantisme suivi de notices romantiques*

friend, Frédéric Villot, suggested that "autant sa peinture était fougueuse, autant sa logique était serrée, froide même, et ce serait une des choses les plus intéressantes de mes révélations que l'exposition de ses théories qu'il ne mettait pas toujours en pratique, il faut l'avouer, lorsqu'il prenait le pinceau."[6] Thus, the spirited warmth and fire of the paintings are contrasted with an alleged frigidity and dryness of theory; practice and theory are dichotomized into mutually exclusive aspects of the artist's personality as though he were truly schizophrenic.

This attitude has survived in our century. Raymond Escholier, aware of the notable difference in tone between the exuberance of the early entries of the Journal of 1822-24 and (after a hiatus in production of twenty-three years) the relative sobriety of the later ones of 1847-63, exalts his subject as the foremost French Romantic, one whose Classical tendencies derived from the understandable fatigue of old age: "On sourit, quand on pense que, se basant sur certaines déclarations d'Eugène Delacroix, vieilli et aspirant alors, en effet, à la sérénité classique, plusieurs biographes oubliant simplement toute l'œuvre de jeunesse de Delacroix, Faust et Sardanapale, lui ont dénié son premier titre de gloire, celui que lui décernèrent bon gré mal gré, ses contemporains, ses amis, les Silvestre et les Baudelaire, son titre de chef de l'école de peinture romantique."[7] And Lionello Venturi, seeking motivation for the frequent disparity between Delacroix's free, spontaneous technique in his painted sketches and his relatively sedate manner in finished works, suggested that the source of this change lay in the traditional aspects of the artist's theory — aspects cultivated allegedly as part of his social *persona*: "His inner ideal being entirely an aspiration to romantic boldness, his work turned out to be less romantic through its adherence, albeit sincere, to an exterior ideal — to a social façade, even though unconsciously so. Rather than romantic in spite of classical reasoning, his painting can be considered in-

---

et d'une étude sur la poésie française, *1830-1868*, Paris, 1895, p. 205. (1st ed., 1874.)

[6] From a letter of July 27, 1869, from Frédéric Villot to Alfred Sensier; quoted by Maurice Tourneux, *Eugène Delacroix devant ses contemporains*, Paris, 1886, p. 124.

[7] Raymond Escholier, *Delacroix: peintre, graveur, écrivain*, Paris, 1926, I, p. 116.

completely romantic because of classical reasoning."[8] In this view, the art of Delacroix suffered diminution of the Romantic temperature under the chilling influence of alien philosophy.

These interpretations not only are based upon an oversimplified theory of clear distinction between Classical and Romantic modes of expression but they fail to do justice to the subtlety and complexity of Delacroix's intellect. Other writers, aware of the profoundly interrelated nature of the Classical and Romantic tendencies of early nineteenth-century art, have come closer to the heart of the matter. Baudelaire, ever percipient, had already given the essential clue in 1863 when he described Delacroix as "passionnément amoureux de la passion, et froidement déterminé à chercher les moyens d'exprimer la passion de la manière la plus visible."[9] In 1928, Paul Jamot linked Delacroix with Baudelaire in this respect: "Comme Delacroix, Baudelaire est à la fois romantique et classique."[10] Lucien Rudrauf, in his probing account of the artist's aesthetic, described the Romantic and the Classical aspects of his theory as complementary rather than exclusive agents, pointing out that "l'irrationnel et le rationnel peuvent prévaloir tour à tour au cours de la gestation d'une œuvre."[11] And, most recently, René Huyghe has aptly described the extraordinary mixture of lucidity and ineffability to be found in Delacroix's art: "A great part of him was fascinated by this miraculous power of conjuring up and conveying emotionally what cannot be expressed in words. Yet his nature was too complex and rich for him to abandon himself to this entirely. Strengthened by a solid classicist

[8] Lionello Venturi, "Delacroix," *L'Arte*, new series, II, 1931, pp. 64-65. Victor Hugo, in 1863, anticipated the attitude of Venturi when he wrote: "Le jeune chef du mouvement en peinture n'avait pas le même audace en paroles qu'en tableaux. Il tâchait de désarmer, par les concessions de sa conversation, les ennemis que lui faisait l'originalité de son admirable talent. Révolutionnaire dans son atelier, il était conservateur dans les salons, reniait toute solidarité avec les idées nouvelles, désavouait l'insurrection littéraire et préférait la tragédie au drame." Victor Hugo, "Victor Hugo raconté par un témoin de sa vie," *Œuvres complètes de Victor Hugo*, Paris, 1885, XLVIII, p. 239. (1st ed., 1863, published under the name of Madame Adèle Victor Hugo.)

[9] Charles Baudelaire, "L'Œuvre et la vie d'Eugène Delacroix," *Curiosités esthétiques, L'Art romantique et autres œuvres critiques de Baudelaire*, ed. Henri Lemaitre, Paris, 1962, p. 426.

[10] Jamot, *op.cit.*, p. 103.

[11] Lucien Rudrauf, *Eugène Delacroix et le problème du romantisme artistique*, Paris, 1942, p. 11.

education, the Latin was still there in him: he meant to go beyond
it but not to give it up, and he refused to allow himself an abdica-
tion of order and lucidity."[12]

The present study naturally endeavors first of all to identify
many sources of Delacroix's art theory — to bring to light in a systematic manner the astonishingly wide range of his acquaintanceship with past and contemporary writings on art including those
of Horace, Longinus, Leonardo da Vinci, Lodovico Dolce, Benvenuto Cellini, Poussin, Boileau, Roger de Piles, Joseph Addison,
Sir Joshua Reynolds, Diderot, Madame de Staël, Stendhal, and Baudelaire. In the process of elucidation the various strands of the
closely interwoven texture of traditional and original theory shine
forth in greater clarity and it is possible to disentangle ideas hereto-
fore accepted as Delacroix's own.[13] Beyond these immediate results,
however, there emerges support for the position of those who find no
conflict between his art and his theory and stress integration rather
than dichotomy in his rational and irrational tendencies. During
the course of this study, as we shall discover, there develops an un-
mistakable pattern of motivation and preference in his citation
and adaptation of theoretical material from other writers — a pattern which suggests that he was striving for a reintegration of
reason and passion in the creative act and in the human personality. Armed with a formidable wealth of knowledge of past theory,
he clearly divined the pitfalls facing an art exclusively dependent
upon either human faculty. In so doing he met the major challenge
of post-Renaissance art. This challenge has been attributed by the
eminent critic of the theater, Francis Fergusson, to a breach in the
human personality — a breach which opened in the seventeenth
century when reason assumed primacy as the existential instrument, a breach unhealed when, in extreme reaction, passion
triumphed in the nineteenth century. Consequently, "the theaters
of Racine and Wagner are . . . arbitrary inventions and the image
they reflect — images of reason or passion — are artificially limited, and thus, in a sense even false."[14] At the conclusion of this

[12] René Huyghe, *Delacroix*, New York, 1963, p. 198. Also, for Delacroix's
response to traditional art and ideas, see Marc Le Bot, "Delacroix et la tradition," *Europe: revue mensuelle*, April 1963, pp. 22-34.
[13] See below, pp. 30-31 and nn. 72, 73, 74.
[14] Francis Fergusson, *The Idea of a Theater*, Princeton, 1949, p. 3. The ap-

study it should be abundantly clear that Delacroix struggled — in his art and in his theory — to repair this breach and to reconcile once more reason and passion, the Classical and the Romantic.

pearance of this dichotomy in the seventeenth century has also been described by Walter Jackson Bate, *From Classic to Romantic: Premises of Taste in Eighteenth Century England*, New York, 1961, pp. 43-44: "The dichotomy which the neo-classic rationalist had tended to make between 'reason' and any aspect whatsoever of imagination and feeling had become sufficiently prevalent so that those who urged another basis for taste were often equally extreme in maintaining emotion as its primary foundation, and in viewing 'reason' and the employment of the rules as almost its opposite."

CHAPTER I

DELACROIX'S CONCEPTION

OF ART

ONE OF THE most remarkable aspects of Delacroix's personality was an extraordinary need for articulation in all matters that concerned his art — a need that found ample outlet in his Journal, correspondence, and the numerous articles published in various periodicals of the time.[1] The patient reader of this abundant lit-

[1] Fundamental to any study of Delacroix's writings are the monumental editions of his *Journal* and *Correspondance* edited by André Joubin: *Journal d'Eugène Delacroix*, 3 vols., Paris, 1960 (a reprint of the edition of 1932 with a new introduction by Jean-Louis Vaudoyer) and *Correspondance générale d'Eugène Delacroix*, 2d ed., 5 vols., Paris, 1936-38. Henceforth, *Journal* and *Correspondance générale* will refer to these editions. These volumes have superseded earlier publications of Delacroix's notes and letters, notably (in the case of the *Journal*) Paul Flat (ed.), *Journal d'Eugène Delacroix*, 3 vols., Paris, 1893-95 and (in the case of the letters) J.-J. Guiffrey (ed.), *Lettres inédites d'Eugène Delacroix*, Paris, 1877, and Philippe Burty, *Lettres d'Eugène Delacroix*, Paris, 1878 (of which there is a second edition enlarged, Paris, 1880). Two English translations of the *Journal* have been published: one by Walter Pach, *The Journal of Eugène Delacroix*, New York, 1937, and another by Lucy Norton, *The Journal of Eugène Delacroix*, London, 1951. Both translations offer only excerpts from their rich source thereby diluting their value for the serious student of Delacroix's thought. Pach's translation lacks the elementary convenience of an index. Important additions to the corpus of the artist's correspondence have been assembled by A. Dupont (ed.), *Eugène Delacroix: lettres intimes, correspondance inédite*, Paris, 1954. Also essential to this study is the collection of Delacroix's published articles (including additional notes): Elie Faure (ed.), *Eugène Delacroix: Œuvres littéraires*, 2 vols., Paris, 1923. Henceforth, *Œuvres littéraires* will refer to this edition. These volumes, though inadequately edited, supersede two early attempts to collect this material: E. A. Piron, *Eugène Delacroix: sa vie et ses œuvres*, Paris, 1865, and G. Dargenty, *Eugène Delacroix par lui-même*, Paris, 1885. One of these articles, "Des critiques en matière d'art," has been translated by Walter Pach as *On Art Criticism*, N.Y., 1946. Selections from Delacroix's writings in all forms have been assembled in *Ecrits d'Eugène Delacroix: Extraits du journal, des lettres et des œuvres littéraires*, published under the direction of Jacques and René

erary production will be rewarded with a literate and penetrating introduction to something approaching the entire range of subject matter treated by art theoreticians from antiquity to the nineteenth century. The definition of art, the aim of painting, the role of imitation, the nature of the creative process, and the disposition of various elements of the finished product, both general and specific, are all explored here with the insight of one who coupled an ample knowledge of past writings on art theory with intimate, practical experience as a painter. Significantly, he was not content with the casual nature of the greater part of his written comments on these matters, especially those scattered throughout his Journal and his letters. During a lengthy illness in 1857 he recorded a desire to formalize his views with an initial sketch of a proposed *Dictionnaire des beaux-arts* which, unfortunately, was never completed.[2] In addition to this abortive attempt he ambitiously envisioned another work — of less fragmentary form — which would present a more unified exposition of his aesthetics: "Il faut de toutes mes notes, autres que celles qui s'appliquent au *Dictionnaire*, faire un ouvrage suivi, au moyen de la jonction des passages analogues et au moyen de transitions insensibles. Il ne faut donc pas les détacher et les publier séparément. Par exemple, mettre ensemble tout ce qui est du spectacle de la nature, etc."[3] This, too, was destined to remain unaccomplished.[4] Together, these works would no doubt have rivaled the encyclopedic authority of Leonardo da Vinci's *Treatise on Painting*. But, in actuality, it is per-

---

Wittmann, 2 vols., Paris, 1942. Recently, Delacroix's youthful efforts as a creative writer have been noted by Jean Marchand, in "Delacroix fut écrivain avant d'être peintre," *Les Nouvelles Littéraires*, August 14, 1952, and in his edition of one of Delacroix's efforts as a creative writer, *Les dangers de la cour*, Avignon, 1960.

2 The entries in the Journal for January 11, 13, 23, 25 and February 4 are especially rewarding for samples of the contents of the projected *Dictionnaire*. See *Journal*, III, pp. 9-62.

3 *Journal*, III, pp. 42-43 (January 25, 1857).

4 Perhaps the reason for his failure to achieve the essay lay in his distaste for expanded literary forms as expressed on November 1, 1852: "Qu'un homme de talent, qui veut fixer ses pensées sur les arts, les répande à mesure qu'elles lui viennent; qu'il ne craigne pas de se contredire, il y'aura plus de fruit à recueillir au milieu de la profusion de ses idées, même contradictoires, que dans la trame peignée, resserrée, découpée d'un ouvrage dans lequel la forme l'aura occupé . . ." *Journal*, I, p. 496. On this matter see Claude Roger-Marx, "Le plus grand des critiques d'art," René Huyghe *et al.*, *Delacroix*, Paris, 1963, pp. 205-24.

haps just as well that the kernels of his wisdom must be sought by the modern reader throughout scattered pages of his writings. For, unlike Leonardo, in whom even the profoundest meditations upon the nature of art partake of the clear, steady vision of the High Renaissance, Delacroix manifests an altogether more modern complexity that benefits from a fragmentary presentation. So it is that he can offer various, often contradictory, interpretations of any given subject matter. And, in a sense, this lack of formal completion takes on a very positive value since it allows him to avoid the dogmatic narrowness inherent in most final statements. Indeed, this lack of dogma serves as a symbol of the nature of his thought which, as we shall discover, usually preferred to appreciate the advantages of all approaches to art, especially those which historians have dichotomized into the poles of Romanticism and Classicism.

THE DEFINITION OF PAINTING

Evidence of this awareness of the fundamental problems involving art theory and of his ability to investigate alternative solutions can be found in his attempt to formulate a practical and reasonable definition of painting. In the Journal, he reports a conversation of April 1849, with his close and sympathetic friend Chopin, with whom he evolved a definition of art. It poses a problem for those writers who regard him as a pure Romantic. Inspired by Chopin's remarks on the use of harmony and counterpoint in order to establish a sense of order and logic in music, he decided that art and science were not necessarily contrary phenomena. "Non," he wrote, "la science envisagée ainsi, démontrée par un homme comme Chopin, est l'art lui-même, et par contre l'art n'est plus alors ce que le croit le vulgaire, c'est-à-dire une sorte d'inspiration qui vient de je ne sais où, qui marche au hasard, et ne présente que l'extérieur pittoresque des choses. C'est la raison elle-même ornée par le génie, mais suivant une marche nécessaire et contenue par des lois supérieures."[5] Art, then, is a manifestation of reason (although embellished by genius); it is a science and not a matter of irrational inspiration; it follows the path of necessity guided by

[5] *Journal*, I, p. 284 (April 7, 1849).

authoritative rule. How different from those Romantic definitions which usually revel in splendid but vague effusions![6]

By dissociating himself, on this occasion, from the Romantic view of art, Delacroix harked back to traditional conceptions that flourished during the Renaissance and the period of the Baroque. His linking of art and the rational processes was anticipated in 1436 by Leon Battista Alberti, who, taking the ancient painter Pamphilos as his guide, characterized geometry as the very basis of art and claimed that "one who is ignorant in geometry will not understand . . . any other rules of painting."[7] Leonardo da Vinci, in his *Treatise on Painting* (a work known by Delacroix), enlisted painting among the sciences in no uncertain terms: "Truly this is a science and the legitimate daughter of nature, since painting is born of nature. To speak more accurately, we would say the grandchild of nature, for all visible things are born of nature, and painting is born of these."[8]

This conception of painting as the rendering of "visible things" in a scientific manner found its way into French Academic theory

[6] Take, for one, the example of Baudelaire who claimed that "la peinture est une évocation, une opération magique (si nous pouvions consulter là-dessus l'âme des enfants!), et quand le personnage évoqué, quand l'idée ressuscitée, se sont dressés et nous ont regardés face à face, nous n'avons pas le droit, — du moins ce serait le comble de la puérilité, — de discuter les formules évocatoires du sorcier." From his review of the *Exposition universelle* of 1855; see Charles Baudelaire, *Curiosités esthétiques* . . . , p. 217.

[7] Leon Battista Alberti, *On Painting*, tr. John R. Spencer, New Haven, 1956, p. 90. According to Pliny, Pamphilos, the master of Apelles, "was the first painter who was thoroughly trained in every branch of learning, more particularly in arithmetic and geometry; without which, so he held, art could not be perfect." See K. Jex-Blake and E. Sellers, *The Elder Pliny's Chapters on the History of Art*, London, 1896, p. 119.

[8] Leonardo da Vinci, *Treatise on Painting*, tr. A. P. McMahon, Princeton, 1956, I, p. 5. On April 3, 1860, Delacroix noted that he had recently read a life of Leonardo by M. Clément, which had appeared in the *Revue des Deux-Mondes* (see M. Clément, "Léonard de Vinci," *Revue des Deux-Mondes*, XXVI, April, 1860, pp. 603-43). This work inspired him to remark: "Ce serait un ouvrage curieux qu'un commentaire sur le traité de la peinture de Léonard. Broder sur cette sécheresse donnerait matière à tout ce qu'on voudrait." *Journal*, III, p. 284. Whether he knew Leonardo's work at first hand is difficult to ascertain. His remark concerning its "dryness" suggests that he did. In any case, three translations of this work were available by the first half of the nineteenth century: one by Roland Fréart Sieur de Chambray, *Traité de la peinture de Léonard de Vinci*, Paris, 1651; another, *Traité de la peinture par Léonard de Vinci*, Paris, 1716, which was reprinted in 1796 and 1803; the third, *Traité de la peinture par Léonard de Vinci*, tr. P. M. Gault de St. Germain, Paris, 1803, reprinted in Geneva, 1820.

as articulated by André Félibien, who in 1676 considered painting "un art qui par des lignes, et des couleurs représente sur une surface égale et unie tous les objets de la nature" and reason as "le père de la peinture."[9] In the eighteenth century reason still held sway in one of Delacroix's favorite authors, Montesquieu,[10] who stated in his *Essai sur le goût*: "J'ai dit souvent que ce qui nous fait plaisir doit être fondé sur la raison; et ce qui ne l'est pas à certains égards, mais parvient à nous plaire par d'autres, doit s'en écarter le moins qu'il est possible."[11]

One year later, in the Journal, Delacroix demonstrated his flexibility as an art theorist by proposing a conception of painting that differs radically from the conservative one he developed with Chopin. It is also one that has found a more enthusiastic response from those critics who emphasize the Romantic aspect of his art. Here he seems to abandon the rational basis of the arts for one that stresses its irrational roots: "Je me suis dit cent fois," he wrote in 1850, "que la peinture, c'est-à-dire la peinture matérielle, n'était que le prétexte, que le pont entre l'esprit du peintre et celui du spectateur. La froide exactitude n'est pas l'art; l'ingénieux artifice, quand il *plaît* ou qu'il *exprime*, est l'art tout entier."[12] We are, with this statement, no longer in the world of Renaissance and Baroque theory; rather, it belongs to the main stream of Romanticism. Art now is not an end in itself but chiefly a bridge or means of communication between painter and spectator; moreover, it communicates warmth of expression rather than cold and exact copies of visual reality. No wonder Baudelaire admired this Ro-

[9] André Félibien, *Des principes de l'architecture, de la sculpture, de la peinture*, 3d ed., Paris, 1697, p. 288. (1st ed., 1676.)

[10] For example, on October 9, 1849, Delacroix remarked: "Passé la matinée à lire Montesquieu." *Journal*, I, p. 314.

[11] From Montesquieu's *Essai sur le goût dans les choses de la nature et de l'art* (published posthumously in 1757 as part of the article *Goût* in the *Encyclopédie ou dictionnaire raisonné des sciences, des arts, et des métiers*, ed. D. Diderot and J. L. d'Alembert, 1751-65); see *Œuvres complètes de Montesquieu*, Paris, 1823, V, p. 201.

[12] *Journal*, I, p. 391 (July 18, 1850). Delacroix's objection to "cold exactitude" can be interpreted as part of his reaction to David and his school. According to Delacroix, this quality of coldness was characteristic not only of David's art but also his personality. "L'asservissement complet à ce que lui présentait le modèle est une des causes de cette froideur: mais il est plus juste de penser que cette froideur était en lui-même . . ." *Journal*, III, p. 70 (March 5, 1857).

mantic posture when he suggested that "en un mot, Eugène Delacroix peint surtout l'*âme* dans ses belles heures."[13]

It must be emphasized, however, that even in this definition that expresses the aims of a more contemporary mode of artistic creation Delacroix was not at all a pioneer. Already in 1765 another of his favorite authors, Denis Diderot, had outlined its fundamental premise when, speaking of a painting entitled *Russian Pastorale* by Jean-Baptiste le Prince (1734-81), he claimed that "que m'importent tes passages de tons savants, ton dessin pur et correct, la vigueur de ton coloris, la magie de ton clair-obscur, si ton sujet me laisse froid? La peinture est l'art d'aller à l'âme par l'entremise des yeux. Si l'effet s'arrête aux yeux, le peintre n'a fait que la moindre partie du chemin."[14] Moreover, it is clear that, for Diderot, the content of painting resided in the "soul" since he once wrote: ". . . cette imitation, où en est le modèle? dans l'âme, dans l'esprit, dans l'imagination plus ou moins vive, dans le cœur plus ou moins chaud de l'auteur."[15] This insistence upon the warmth of the subject and upon the role of the painting as a vehicle for the communication between souls announces already the spirit of Romanticism. It was such statements as these that nourished the mind of Delacroix and must account for his avid interest in the works of Diderot. The influence of Diderot in this matter remained a lasting one for, seven years later (January 25, 1857), as part of his

[13] From Baudelaire's Salon of 1859; see *Curiosités esthétiques* . . . , p. 341.

[14] From Diderot's Salon of 1765; see *Œuvres complètes de Diderot*, ed. J. Assézat, Paris, 1876, x, p. 376. Various writers have noted the importance of Diderot for Delacroix's art theory; see especially André Joubin, *Correspondance générale*, I, pp. 290-91, n. 1; Jean Seznec, in *Diderot Salons*, ed. J. Seznec and J. Adhémar, Oxford, 1957, I, pp. 1-25; and Gita May, *Diderot et Baudelaire: critiques d'art*, Paris, 1957, pp. 27-37. The breadth of Delacroix's acquaintanceship with the works of Diderot was remarkable. He knew the *Paradox of Acting*: "Parlé de l'opinion de Diderot sur le comédien." (*Journal*, I, p. 170; January 27, 1847.) In a letter to a friend he requested the loan of a publication of Diderot's correspondence: "Mon cher Ricourt, pouvez-vous m'avoir la *Correspondance* de Diderot. Il y a là-dedans matière plus qu'il n'en faut à vous brocher quelques articles sur les arts." (*Correspondance générale*, I, pp. 290-91; letter of August 2, 1831.) And as early as 1821, if Joubin's dating of the letter is correct, Delacroix requested from his friend, Jean-Baptiste Pierret, a copy of Diderot's *Essai sur le peinture*: "Tu me ferais plaisir d'apporter ton volume de Diderot et d'y joindre s'il est possible l'*Essai sur la peinture*. On me l'a perdu depuis longtemps et je grille de le lire." (*Correspondance générale*, I, p. 108.)

[15] From Diderot's *Pensées détachées*; see Denis Diderot, *Essais sur la peinture*, ed. Roland Desné, Paris, 1955, pp. 202-3.

preparatory notes for the projected *Dictionnaire*, he repeats this theme utilizing now Diderot's term, *l'âme*: "La source principale de l'intérêt [in a work of art] vient de l'âme, et elle va à l'âme du spectateur d'une manière irrésistible. . . ."[16]

THE AIM OF PAINTING

These statements constitute not only definitions of painting; they also serve to inform the reader of Delacroix's conception of the primary aim of art: to function as a bridge between the soul of the artist and the soul of the spectator.

The latter half of this proposition, that it was the soul of the spectator which offered the essential target for the painter, is not in itself a Romantic innovation. Beginning with the Renaissance it boasts a continuous history as the object of painterly endeavors. For, although Renaissance theory never advocated the expression of the artist's subjective feeling, it can be demonstrated that, beginning as early as the fifteenth century, the soul of the spectator was a continuous preoccupation of writers on art. Alberti, in his *Della pittura*, stresses the importance of moving the soul of the spectator.[17] And Lodovico Dolce, in his *Dialogo della pittura intitolato l'Aretino* of 1557, a work which Delacroix knew, speaks of moving the soul of the spectator in a passage that also warns against the lack of warmth in a work of art: "Enfin on recherche, dans le peintre une autre qualité, qui si elle manque à sa peinture, son ouvrage devient froid, et ses figures semblent mortes, et sans aucun mouvement. C'est qu'il faut, que les figures remuent l'esprit des spectateurs, les unes en les troublant, d'autres en les rejouissant, celles-ci les émouvant à compassion, celles-là les portant à la colère, selon la qualité de l'histoire."[18]

16 *Journal*, III, p. 48. For further discussion of Diderot as a precursor of Romanticism see especially: Margaret Gilman, "Imagination and Creation in Diderot," *Diderot Studies*, ed., O. E. Fellows and N. L. Torrey, Syracuse, 1949-52, II, pp. 200-20; and "The Poet According to Diderot," *Romantic Review*, XXXVII (February 1946), pp. 37-54. See also the introduction by Jean Seznec in *Diderot Salons*, I, pp. 1-25.

17 "The *istoria* will move the soul of the beholder when each man painted there clearly shows the movement of his own soul." Leon Battista Alberti, *On Painting*, p. 77.

18 Lodovico Dolce, *Dialogue sur la peinture, intitulé l'Aretin*, Florence, 1735, p. 227. This edition includes the text in both French and Italian. In Italian, the passage reads: "Finalmente ricerca al Pittore un'altra parte: della quale la

This concern for the effect of a work of art upon the soul of the spectator became widespread in the next century. Nicolas Poussin, according to André Félibien, was interested in the way the composition, expression, and color of a painting might achieve the same influence upon the soul as the elements of music.[19] In the field of literature there occurs a discussion of this problem by that arch-Classicist Boileau. This was cited by Delacroix, a great admirer of his work.[20] The passage derives from a letter to Charles Perrault on the lively controversy of the Ancients versus the Moderns.[21] In it, Boileau distinguishes the effect of the tragedies of Corneille from those of the Ancients which had aimed to move the spectator to Aristotelian pity and terror. Instead, according to Boileau, Corneille proposed "à exciter dans l'âme des spectateurs, par la sublimité des pensées, et par la beauté des sentiments, une certaine admiration. . . ."[22] On this occasion, of course, Delacroix's quotation, which appears without any comment, concerns not so much the appeal of the work to the emotions of the spectator as to an exalted sense of admiration induced by sublime thoughts and beautiful sentiments. His interest in this passage can be attributed

---

Pittura, ch'è priva, riman, come si dice, fredda, è a guisa di corpo morto, che non opera cosa veruna. Questo è, che bisogna, che le figure movano gli animi de' riguardanti, alcune turbandogli, altre rallegrandogli, altre sospingendogli a pietà, e altre a sdegno, secondo la qualità della historia." *Ibid.*, p. 226.

[19] Félibien tells us that "de sorte que considérant que la diférence des sons cause à l'âme des mouvements diférens, selon qu'elle est touchée par des tons graves ou aigus, il [Poussin] ne doutoit pas que la manière d'exposer les objets dans une disposition de mouvemens, et une apparence d'expressions plus ou moins violentes, et sous des couleurs mises les unes auprès des autres et mélangées diversement, ne donnât à la vûë diverses sensations qui pouvoient rendre l'âme susceptible d'autant de passions diférentes." André Félibien, *Conférences de l'académie royale de peinture et de sculpture*, London, 1705, preface, pp. 22-23.

[20] *Journal*, III, p. 113 (August 3, 1857). Delacroix's interest in the work and ideas of Boileau was intense. Joubin cites thirteen references to the author in the *Journal*. On August 30, 1859, Delacroix paid tribute to him in these terms: "Boileau est un homme qu'il faut avoir sous son chevet, il délecte et purifie: il fait aimer le beau et l'honnête, tandis que nos modernes n'exhalent que d'âcres parfums, mortels parfois pour l'âme et faussant l'imagination par des spectacles de fantaisie." *Journal*, III, p. 231.

[21] Charles Perrault had attacked the supremacy of Ancient art in his *Parallèles des anciens et des modernes en ce qui regarde les arts et les sciences*, Paris, 1688. For this controversy, see especially: E. Rigault, *Histoire de la querelle des anciens et des modernes*, Paris, 1856; A. Fontaine, *Les doctrines d'art en France de Poussin à Diderot*, Paris, 1909; and H. Gillot, *La querelle des anciens et des modernes en France*, Paris, 1914.

[22] See *Œuvres complètes de Boileau Despréaux*, Paris, 1835, p. 381.

to his general distaste for a contemporary manifestation in art — the Realist Movement — which explicitly avoided those qualities Boileau had discerned in Corneille. This distaste is evident, for one example, in his hostile reaction to Courbet's *Bathers* of 1853 (Fig. 3): "Quel tableau! quel sujet! la vulgarité des formes ne ferait rien; c'est la vulgarité et l'inutilité de la pensée qui sont abominables. . . ."[23]

With so much previous concern for the soul as the object of artistic effort it is not surprising to discover an ever-increasing crescendo of approval of this idea in the proto-Romantic theory of the eighteenth century. Already in the early part of the century (1719), Jean-Baptiste Dubos declared that the soul harbored needs that required attention as urgently as those of the body.[24] Moreover, he anticipated Diderot and Delacroix in their conception of art as a bridge between painter and spectator, surpassing both in his emphasis on the emotional content of art: "La copie de l'objet doit . . . exciter en nous une copie de la passion que l'objet y auroit exciter."[25] And even earlier, an author very familiar to Delacroix, Roger de Piles,[26] claimed for painting at least equal power with the theater to move the public to tears.[27]

This tendency on the part of eighteenth-century writers to equate the soul exclusively with the seat of emotion and to demand of art the stimulation of overt emotion as its chief purpose did not find its way into Delacroix's theory in a pure form. His constant preoccupation with the role of reason no doubt prevented his un-

---

23 *Journal*, II, p. 18 (April 15, 1853). Yet he recognized Courbet's talent as a painter; see *Journal*, II, p. 364 (August 3, 1855) where he praises the *Atelier du peintre* as "un des ouvrages les plus singuliers de ce temps. . . ."

24 "L'âme a ses besoins comme le corps, et l'un des plus grands besoins de l'homme est celui d'avoir l'esprit occupé." Jean Baptiste Dubos, *Réflexions critiques sur la poésie et sur la peinture*, Paris, 1719, I, p. 6.

25 *Ibid.*, p. 25.

26 De Piles' famous "Balance des peintres" once inspired Delacroix to envision a balance of much wider scope: "On pourrait refaire pour tous les beaux ouvrages restés dans la mémoire des hommes ce que de Piles fait pour les peintres seulement." *Journal*, I, p. 344 (February 24, 1850).

27 "Pour les effets que la Poësie et la Peinture font sur les esprits, il est certain que l'une et l'autre sont capables de remuer puissamment les passions, et si les bonnes pièces de théâtre ont tiré et tirent encore tous les jours des larmes de leurs Spectateurs, la Peinture peut faire la même chose quand le sujet le demande, et qu'il est, comme nous le supposons, bien exprimé." Roger de Piles, *Cours de peinture par principes*, Paris, 1708, p. 442.

critical acceptance of this idea. Moreover, a more recent development of the conception of the soul — a more Romantic and, at the same time, more metaphysical interpretation — had evolved in Germany and reached him via another of his favorite sources, Madame de Staël. As early as 1824, the year he submitted *Massacre at Chios* to the Salon, the young artist acknowledged an enormous debt to the influential Frenchwoman for crucial aspects of his theory when he wrote in his Journal: "Je retrouve justement dans Mme de Staël le développement de mon idée sur la peinture."[28] It was in *De l'Allemagne*, which Delacroix knew,[29] that Madame de Staël, inspired by German philosophers and aestheticians,[30] stated a fully developed conception of the subjective origins and aims of art. In her view, art is the vehicle par excellence for the communication of the soul's message: "Le poëte ne fait, pour ainsi dire, que dégager le sentiment prisonnier au fond de l'âme; le génie poétique est une disposition intérieure, de la même nature que celle qui rend capable d'un généreux sacrifice; c'est rêver l'héroïsme que de composer une belle ode."[31] At the same time, however, and this may have influenced Delacroix's rejection of the purely emotive interpretation, she endows the soul with the power to generate ideas as well as feelings: "L'âme est un foyer qui rayonne dans tous les sens; c'est dans ce foyer que consiste l'existence; toutes les observations et tous les efforts des philosophes doivent se tourner vers ce *moi*, centre et mobile de nos sentiments et de nos idées."[32]

It should be clear, then, that when Delacroix described painting as a bridge of communication between souls he invented nothing new; rather, from the rich storehouse of previous ideas on the sub-

[28] *Journal*, I, p. 50 (January 26, 1824).

[29] A long passage given in the *Œuvres littéraires*, I, pp. 65-67, as Delacroix's own is actually a quotation from the *De l'Allemagne*, Paris, 1869, pp. 479-80. (1st ed., 1810.)

[30] For the German origins of the Romantic conception of art embodied in *De l'Allemagne*, see especially Arthur O. Lovejoy, "Schiller and the Genesis of German Romanticism," *Modern Language Notes*, xxxv (January 1920), pp. 1-10 and *ibid.* (March 1920), pp. 136-46, and "On the Discrimination of Romanticisms," *PMLA*, xxxix, 1924, pp. 229-53. Also helpful are E. Ollion, *Les idées philosophiques, morales et pédagogiques de Madame de Staël*, Macon, 1910; Emma Gertrude Jaeck, *Madame de Staël and the Spread of German Literature*, New York, 1915; and Ian Allan Henning, *L'Allemagne de Mme de Staël et la polémique romantique*, Paris, 1929.

[31] De Staël, *op.cit.*, p. 162.

[32] *Ibid.*, pp. 417-18.

ject he selected, in authors with whom he was familiar, a definition by Diderot which did not conflict with a theory he already had considered in the writings of Madame de Staël.

THE SUBLIME

When Delacroix cited Boileau's characterization of Corneille's aim in the writing of tragedy he gave evidence of another of his major preoccupations in the realm of traditional art theory — the sublime, that concept which exalted grandeur, nobility of thought, imagination, and emotion as principal elements of art. There exists ample evidence that he was well acquainted not only with Boileau's conception but also with various amplifications of the idea which had developed in England, France, and Germany. Furthermore, this interest no doubt influenced his art and may account for certain of its aspects which have puzzled critics who look to him only for turbulent themes expressed in terms of symphonic color.

The sublime had been intimately connected with the soul in its first formulation by Longinus, who insisted that its primary purpose was to elevate the soul. Delacroix, who abhorred what he considered trivial subject matter (especially as manifested in the works of Courbet) and who always entertained an exalted opinion of his own contribution to the history of French painting, actually quoted from Boileau's translation of Longinus' *On the Sublime* a passage that describes its elevating properties: "Car tout ce qui est véritablement sublime a cela de propre, quand on l'écoute, qu'il élève l'âme et lui fait concevoir une plus haute opinion d'elle-même, la remplissant de joie et de je ne sais quel noble orgueil: comme si c'était elle qui eût produit les choses qu'elle vient simplement d'entendre."[33] How appropriate a citation this is for an artist who, during the very period of the genesis of the Realist Movement, had, in his vast and monumental works of the 1840's, covered the ceilings of public buildings in Paris with such uplifting themes as *Parnassus* at the Library of the Palais de Luxembourg (1846), *Apollo Destroying the Serpent Python* in the Gallery

[33] *Journal*, III, p. 230 (August 25, 1859). For the source of this quotation, see *Œuvres complètes de Boileau Despréaux*, p. 325. For the Longinian source, see Longinus, *On the Sublime*, tr. W. Hamilton Fyfe, London, 1927, p. 139.

of Apollo of the Louvre (1850), and *Orpheus Bringing Civilization to the Primitive Greeks* of the Library of the Palais Bourbon (1843-47, Fig. 1).

Further interest in the sublime probably derived from his acute awareness of his own creative gift as a talent not always at the highest peak of inspiration and achievement. During June 1847, he contemplated the writing of an article on the sublime,[34] and he became particularly interested in the dictum of Longinus and Boileau which held that the achievement of sublime effects justified concomitant faults and imperfections.[35] And later variations of this theme enriched his treatment of this concept.

During the eighteenth century there developed a habit of using genius as the criterion of the sublime in judging writers of the past. According to this theory, a work of genius may manifest faults and disproportions because of the impressive results achieved.[36] Delacroix frequently adopted this approach, notably in the Journal entry of October 26, 1853, where he took inspiration from one of his favorite authors, Joseph Addison, whose *Spectator* papers he regarded as suitable models in style and format for a projected literary effort of his own.[37] He noted that "le *Spectateur* parle de ce qu'il appelle *génies de premier ordre*, tels que Pindare, Homère, la Bible — confus au milieu de choses sublimes et inachevées, — Shakespeare, etc.; puis de ceux dans lesquels il voit plus d'art, tels que Virgile, Platon, etc."[38] Furthermore, the application of this

---

[34] "Article sur le *Sublime*. Voir dans les notes pour le *Dictionnaire*." *Journal*, III, p. 106.

[35] See *Journal*, III, p. 108 (June 26, 1857). On this matter, see Longinus, *op.cit.*, p. 217. In his *L'Art poétique*, Boileau defended excesses in the work of Juvenal on the basis of his achievement of sublime effects: "Ses ouvrages, tout pleins d'affreuses vérités,/ Etincellent pourtant de sublimes beautés." *Œuvres complètes de Boileau Despréaux*, p. 246.

[36] See, for example, Edward Young who, in his *Conjectures on Original Composition* (1759), cited Pindar and Shakespeare as writers whose attainment of the sublime justifies occasional lapses in taste and judgment. This phenomenon is discussed by Samuel H. Monk in *The Sublime: A Study of Critical Theories in XVIII Century England*, New York, 1935, pp. 101-3.

[37] "Je ne fais que rêver à un ouvrage dans le genre de celui du *Spectateur*: un article court de trois ou quatre pages et de moins encore, sur le premier sujet venu." *Journal*, II, p. 39 (May 8, 1853).

[38] *Journal*, II, p. 102 (October 26, 1853). For more on the problem of genius, see below Chapter III. The notion of imperfection as a condition of the sublime occurs again in a later entry of the Journal: "*Sublime*. J'ai dit que chez les grands hommes dont le sublime semble être l'élément, l'art paraît jouer un rôle secondaire." *Journal*, III, p. 164 (November 30, 1857).

conception more specifically to the realm of painting was advocated by Sir Joshua Reynolds whose *Discourses* had provided a mine of information and inspiration for copious reading notes and comments in the Journal.[39] Reynolds added to the literary Pantheon of flawed but sublime geniuses the inevitable figure from the world of the visual arts, Michelangelo, claiming that "if, as Longinus thinks, the sublime, being the highest excellence that human composition can attain to, abundantly compensates the absence of every other beauty, and atones for all other deficiencies, then Michael Angelo demands the preference."[40] Delacroix echoes this idea in his Journal adding the notion that the genius of Michelangelo and others of his kind — Corneille and Shakespeare — is characteristic of initiators of a style or movement in art: "Que si les génies, incorrects et sublimes en même temps, sont plus sujets à la critique, ils sont plus souvent en général des sortes d'initiateurs, *de précurseurs*, etc. Corneille, Shakespeare, Michel-Ange."[41] And, in another entry of the Journal, during a discussion of the relative merits of the Parthenon and the church of the Madeleine in Paris (the former is "parfait" and the latter "mauvaise"), he restates the traditional conception: "Une proportion trop parfaite nuit à l'impression du *Sublime*."[42]

This abstract theorizing on the subject of the sublime takes on more practical significance in an entry made two weeks later (January 25, 1857). Here Delacroix recalls as an example of the principle that the sublime depends, in part, on lack of proportion, a previous experience (noted in the Journal, May 9, 1853) which revealed that one of his favorite visual subjects — the oak tree of Antin situated in a forest near Champrosay — embodied, under certain conditions, this principle of the sublime: "Je cite dans un Agenda (1853, 9 mai) que *le Chêne* d'Antin vu à distance paraît médiocre. Sa forme est régulière: la masse des feuilles est propor-

[39] In his article on Michelangelo, which appeared in the *Revue de Paris* of 1830, Delacroix quotes Reynolds' famous eulogy of the Italian master which occurs at the end of the final Discourse; see *Œuvres littéraires*, II, pp. 55-56. For important paraphrases by Delacroix from the works of Reynolds see the *Supplément* of the *Journal*, III, pp. 358-59.

[40] From the Fifth Discourse (December 10, 1772); see *Sir Joshua Reynolds: Discourses on Art*, ed. Robert R. Wark, San Marino, 1959, p. 84.

[41] *Journal*, III, p. 153 (November 20, 1857).

[42] *Journal*, III, p. 14 (January 13, 1857).

tionnée au tronc et à l'extension des branches. Arrivé sous les branches mêmes, n'apercevant que des parties sans rapport avec l'ensemble, j'éprouve la sensation du sublime."[43]

Perhaps this conception of the sublime as embodied in a nearby tree, where the impression of the whole is replaced by the sensation of disproportionate parts, found its way into one of Delacroix's greatest works — *Jacob Wrestling with the Angel* of 1854-61 (Fig. 4) . Here the huge, convulsive trees play a major role. Occupying about one-third of the picture space, they extend towards the viewer and demand consideration not as whole entities but rather as an arrangement of separate elements — gnarled trunks, crooked branches, and luxuriant foliage. The resultant effect is fragmentary, disproportionate, and ultimately menacing — just the effect described by Delacroix when he moved close to the oak tree: "Si je me place au-dessous de ses branches, l'impression change complètement: n'apercevant que le tronc auquel je touche presque et la naissance de ses grosses branches, qui s'étendent au-dessus de ma tête comme les immenses bras de ce géant de la forêt, je suis étonné de la grandeur de ses détails, en un mot, je le trouve grand et même effrayant de grandeur."[44] In other words, as Delacroix had noticed in 1857 (a period when he was at work on this painting) one experiences "la sensation du sublime." Furthermore, the exploitation of the "sensation" of the sublime appears especially appropriate as a means of furthering the ultimate goal in his religious works, which he described as the expression of subjective content. "Mais les sujets religieux," he once wrote to a friend, "entre tous les genres d'attrait qu'ils présentent, ont celui de laisser toute carrière à l'imagination, de manière à ce que chacun y trouve à exprimer son sentiment particulier."[45] The "sublime" treescape contributes to the spiritual and imaginative power generated by his visualization of a cosmic battle between human and supernatural forces.

[43] *Journal*, III, p. 37.

[44] *Journal*, II, p. 42 (May 9, 1853). René Huyghe, *Delacroix*, p. 412, has noted the impressive nature of these trees: "A breath from the world of legend seems to be shaping them afresh and changing them into creatures outside circumstance. They are, as Barrès puts it, 'heroized,' to fit in with the feelings of the combatants."

[45] From a letter of October 5, 1850, to his friend, the painter Constant Dutilleux; see *Correspondance générale*, III, p. 37.

DELACROIX'S CONCEPTION OF ART
THE TERRIBLE

When Delacroix spoke of the terrifying aspect of the grandeur of the oak tree of Antin, he established a link between terror and the sublime that can be related to eighteenth-century developments in the history of the idea. For previously, during the seventeenth century, the sublime had been considered a healthy manifestation intended, as Boileau suggested, "à élever et à ravir l'âme, et qui provient . . . de la grandeur de la pensée et de la noblesse du sentiment. . . ."[46] That is to say, it was still controlled by the dictates of reason and designed to appeal to the nobler feelings. However, in the eighteenth century, in the words of Samuel Monk, "the sublime supplanted grace as a repository for the irregular and irrational elements in art. . . ."[47] At the same time, the irrational and subjective element of terror came to be one of its chief attributes.

It was in England, in 1756, that Edmund Burke described terror as "the ruling principle of the sublime" claiming that "whatever is fitted in any sort to excite the ideas of pain and danger, that is to say, whatever is in any sort terrible, or is conversant about terrible objects, or operates in a manner analogous to terror, is a source of the *sublime*; that is, it is productive of the strongest emotion which the mind is capable of feeling."[48] A decade later this conception appeared on the Continent in the works of Diderot who, in his Salon of 1767, proclaimed the new doctrine in these terms: "Tout ce qui étonne l'âme, tout ce qui imprime un sentiment de terreur conduit au sublime,"[49] thus making this concept available to his avid reader Delacroix.

Although we lack evidence that Delacroix knew Burke's writings at first hand, the English writer's modifications of the sublime open new avenues of interpretation of certain aspects of his art. For Burke, in his invitation to the artist "to excite the ideas of pain and danger," thereby rousing terror and, ultimately, the effect of the sublime, specifies certain appropriate subject matter which is re-

[46] From "Réflexions critiques sur quelques passages du rhéteur Longin," *Œuvres complètes de Boileau Despréaux*, p. 380.

[47] Samuel H. Monk, "A Grace Beyond the Reach of Art," *Journal of the History of Ideas*, v (April 1944), p. 150.

[48] Edmund Burke, *A Philosophical Enquiry into the Origin of Our Ideas of the Sublime and Beautiful*, London, 1812, p. 58. (1st ed., 1756.)

[49] *Œuvres complètes de Diderot*, xi, p. 146.

lated to what Baudelaire called the *caractère molochiste* of Delacroix's work[50] and which Mario Praz attributes to the sublimated expression of Delacroix's sex life.[51] Delacroix, indeed, does stress strong degrees of pain, suffering, and torture in a score of pictures beginning with *Dante and Virgil* of 1822 (Fig. 5), continuing through the *Massacre at Chios* of 1824 (Fig. 7) and the *Death of Sardanapalus* of 1827 (Fig. 6), and still present in the late *Heliodorus Driven from the Temple* (1854-61; Fig. 8). Perhaps the most striking examples are those that involve human beings at the mercy of wild beasts — as in the *Lion Mauling a Dead Arab* of 1847 (Fig. 9). Such pictures lend themselves to Freudian interpretation. However, it might be well, when confronted with these powerful images, to ponder the words of Burke on pain and danger as sources of the terrible and the sublime. Pain and danger were, in his words, "productive of the strongest emotion which the mind is capable of feeling."[52] Even more suggestive is his characterization of animals as eminently suitable vehicles of terror: "There are many animals who, though far from being large, are yet capable of raising ideas of the sublime, because they are considered as objects of terror. . . ."[53] From Burke's point of view, then, Delacroix, in his famous pictures of wild beasts (many of small dimensions), achieved the coveted quality of the sublime simply by means of the nature of the subject matter. Furthermore, in such pictures as the *Lion Mauling a Dead Arab*, he added to the terror evoked by the image of a wild animal the depiction of death — which Burke considered even more effective as an instigator of the sublime, claiming that "as pain is stronger in its operation than pleasure, so death is in general a much more affecting idea than pain."[54]

[50] Baudelaire, "L'Œuvre et la vie d'Eugène Delacroix," *Curiosités esthétiques* . . . , pp. 440-41. "La moralité de ses œuvres, si toutefois il est permis de parler de la morale en peinture, porte aussi un caractère molochiste visible. Tout, dans son œuvre, n'est que désolation, massacres, incendies; tout port témoignage contre l'éternelle et incorrigible barbarie de l'homme."

[51] "Hence the 'vieux levain,' the 'fond tout noir à contenter' which he felt within himself, was forced to find some outlet, and found it in his paintings." Mario Praz, *The Romantic Agony*, New York, 1956, p. 140. (1st ed., 1933.)

[52] Burke, *op.cit.*, p. 58. On Delacroix's paintings of beasts, see especially Lucien Rudrauf, "De la bête à l'ange: les étapes de la lutte vitale dans le pensée et l'art d'Eugène Delacroix," *Acta Historiae Artium*, IX, fascicules 3-4, 1963, pp. 295-341.

[53] Burke, *op.cit.*, p. 97.

[54] *Ibid.*, p. 59.

The fact remains, however, that Delacroix's frequent exploitation of subject matter that emphasized pain, terror, agony, and death shows profound involvement in the "Romantic agony" described by Mario Praz. The interesting element which comes to light in relation to this rather sensational Romantic content is his concern to restrain his expression in order to remain within the boundaries of art.

Unlike Baudelaire, who admired and translated the works of Edgar Allan Poe, Delacroix discerned in such works as the *Descent into the Maelstrom* a lack of restraint which seriously marred their effectiveness as works of art: "La sensation du *terrible* et encore moins celle de *l'horrible* ne peuvent se supporter longtemps. Il en est de même du *surnaturel*. Je lis depuis quelques jours une histoire d'Edgar Poe qui est celle de naufragés qui sont pendant cinquante pages dans la position la plus horrible et la plus désespérée: rien n'est plus ennuyeux. On reconnaît là le mauvais goût des étrangers. Les Anglais, les Allemands, tous ces peuples antilatins n'ont pas de littérature parce qu'ils n'ont aucune idée du goût et de la mesure."[55] In view of his enthusiastic admiration for the presentation of similar subject matter in Géricault's *Raft of the Medusa* of 1819 ("Je ne puis exprimer l'admiration qu'il m'inspire.") [56] as well as in his own treatment of it (in, for example, *Shipwreck of Don Juan* of 1840) this statement, considered alone, might seem chauvinistic. But, in the context of his theory, it reflects rather an involvement with the problem of the limits to which art can exploit themes that assault the senses and the emotions while remaining art.

He found support for his castigation of Poe in a quotation he made on November 20, 1857, from a work of one of his favorite authors — Voltaire. In this quotation (taken from the *Discours sur la tragédie*), Voltaire, apropos of Corneille's *Rodogune*, had objected to the elaborate poisoning scene in that work: "Des coups aussi terribles ne doivent pas être prodigués, et il n'appartient pas à tout le monde d'oser les frapper. Ces nouveautés demandent une grande circonspection, et une exécution de maître."[57] Voltaire, still

[55] *Journal*, III, p. 36 (January 25, 1857). [56] *Journal*, I, p. 66 (April 1, 1824).
[57] François Marie Arouet de Voltaire, *Œuvres complètes de Voltaire*, Paris, 1828, III, pp. 382-83. The quotation occurs in the *Journal*, III, p. 152.

quoted by Delacroix, goes on to cite the example of Shakespeare and also raises the problem of time that Delacroix had mentioned in his criticism of Poe: "Plus une action théâtrale est majestueuse ou effrayante, plus elle deviendrait insipide, si elle était souvent répétée; à-peu-près comme les détails des batailles, qui, étant par eux-mêmes ce qu'il y a de plus terrible, deviennent froids et ennuyeux, à force de reparaître souvent dans les histoires."[58] Thus, Voltaire warns against the flagrant exploitation of terrible scenes lest the spectacle become distasteful and, at the same time, indicates that repetition of such effects diminishes the intensity of the original by overstatement.

This concern for the definable and proper limits of shocking subject matter in art has a long and honorable history, parts of which Delacroix undoubtedly knew. For example, Voltaire, in his discussion of Aristotle in the *Questions sur l'Encyclopédie par des amateurs* (a passage known by Delacroix[59]), cites well-known lines from Boileau's *L'Art poétique* which credit the arts with the power to lessen the shock of disagreeable subject matter:

> Il n'est point de serpent ni de monstre odieux,
> Qui par l'art imité ne puisse plaire aux yeux,
> D'un pinceau délicat l'artifice agréable,
> Du plus affreux objet fait un objet aimable:
> Ainsi, pour nous charmer, la tragédie en pleurs,
> D'Œdipe tout sanglant fit parler les douleurs.

Voltaire also quotes a more ancient and more venerable authority for this idea — one which, significantly for the art of Delacroix, raises the issue of the depiction of wild beasts. Aristotle himself, Voltaire points out, had in the fourth chapter of the *Poetics* suggested that "nous voyons avec plaisir dans un tableau des animaux affreux, des hommes morts ou mourans que nous ne regarderions qu'avec chagrin et avec frayeur dans la nature. Plus ils sont bien imités, plus ils nous causent de satisfaction."[60]

---

[58] Voltaire, *op.cit.*, III, p. 383.

[59] See the *Journal*, III, pp. 1-2 (January 1, 1857), where Delacroix cites Voltaire's article on Aristotle's *Poetics* during a discussion of the definition of beauty.

[60] Voltaire, *Questions sur l'Encyclopédie par des amateurs*, Geneva, 1771, I (deuxième partie), pp. 111-12. In Aristotle's words, "Objects which in themselves we view with pain, we delight to contemplate when reproduced with absolute

However, Delacroix seems not to have been reassured by such excellent authorities that a work of art, by reason of its artificial nature, at once removes the sting from the ugly and the terrible. In all probability this view carried to its extreme would have offered even more license to his aesthetic foes, the Realists, in their efforts to record all aspects of visual reality.

Therefore, it comes as no surprise to discover him on December 12, 1856, taking note that Mozart, whose music afforded him constant delight and whom he considered "supérieur à tous par sa forme achevée,"[61] had concluded (in a letter to his father) that music was capable of expressing a full range of passion while remaining recognizable as an art form that pleased and charmed at the same time. From this letter Delacroix quoted the following passage, underscoring what he considered its essential point: "Néanmoins, les passions, violentes ou non, ne doivent jamais être exprimées jusqu'au dégoût, et la musique même dans les situations les plus horribles, *ne doit jamais affecter l'oreille, mais la flatter et la charmer, et par conséquent rester toujours musique.*"[62]

---

fidelity: such as the forms of the most ignoble beasts and of dead bodies." *The Poetics of Aristotle*, ed. and tr. S. H. Butcher, London, 1895, p. 15. This problem is related to the more general one of the depiction of the ugly in art. Another discussion that is suggestive in relation to Delacroix's art (although there is no evidence that Delacroix knew his work) occurs in Lessing's *Laocoon*. Lessing also takes Aristotle's statement as his text: "From the examples given by Aristotle he appears not to include ugliness of form among the disagreeable things which may give pleasure in the imitation. His examples are wild beasts and dead bodies. Wild beasts excite terror even when they are not ugly; and this terror, not their ugliness, may be made to produce sensations of pleasure through imitation. So also of dead bodies. Keenness of sympathy, the dreadful thought of our own annihilation, make a dead body in nature an object of aversion. In the imitation the sense of illusion robs sympathy of its sharpness, and, by the addition of various palliating circumstances, that disturbing element may be entirely banished or so inseparably interwoven with these softening features, that terror is almost lost in desire." Gotthold Ephraim Lessing, *Laocoon*, tr. E. Frothingham, Boston, 1898, p. 155. (1st ed., 1766.) I quote the passage at some length since the specific mention of wild beasts and dead bodies pertains so well to a picture like the *Lion Mauling a Dead Arab* (Fig. 9), and to a sense of "terror . . . almost lost in desire" evident in the oddly sensual and languorous *Indian Woman Gnawed by a Tiger* of 1852 (Fig. 10).

[61] *Journal*, II, p. 25.

[62] *Journal*, II, p. 481. For the source of this quotation see *The Letters of Mozart and his Family*, tr. and ed., E. Anderson, London, 1938, III, p. 1144. Mozart, describing one of Osmin's arias from the *Abduction from the Seraglio*, indicated the manner in which he caused the music to assume a sense of controlled disorder: "For just as a man in such a towering rage oversteps all the

Delacroix's preoccupation with the limits to which an artist might subject his public to the terrible stems from his interest in another aim of painting that he shared with tradition — the proposition that art should please.

This proposition runs as a constant leitmotif through the history of art theory.[63] Art critics, whatever their ultimate point of view, rarely denied pleasure — of the more sensuous or more austere varieties, depending upon the writer — a major role in the effect art was to produce on the spectator. For Aristotle "the end of the fine arts is to give pleasure . . . or rational enjoyment."[64] And although the Horatian dictum that held that art should instruct as well as delight "was accepted axiomatically, if uncritically, by most Renaissance and Baroque critics both of poetry and painting,"[65] there appeared certain writers who reacted against the didactic purpose of art (foreshadowing the Romantic reaction against the moral didacticism of French Revolutionary painting) and who openly proclaimed a hedonistic philosophy of art. Typical is Castelvetro's remark: "What do beginning, middle, and end matter in a poem provided it delights?"[66] And even the very serious Tasso once confessed, "I have spent most of my efforts in attempting to please."[67] Not unexpectedly Lodovico Dolce concurs in this opinion and one can imagine, in the light of what we know of his ideas, that Delacroix would have read with interest the following passage from the

---

bounds of order, moderation and propriety and completely forgets himself, so must the music too forget itself." He then records the cautionary words of advice quoted by Delacroix. In the Journal Delacroix merely paraphrased a note he had made from his direct source for this quotation — an article by S. Scudo, "Wolfgang Mozart et l'opéra de Don Juan," *Revue des Deux Mondes*, I (March 1849), pp. 872-925. The excerpt from Mozart's letter (as correctly pointed out by Delacroix) appears on p. 892. See *Journal*, I, p. 290, where, on April 23, 1849, he had first cited this letter.

[63] See Rensselaer W. Lee, "*Ut Pictura Poesis*: The Humanistic Theory of Painting," *Art Bulletin*, XXII (December 1940), pp. 197-269, especially Section IV (pp. 226-28) which treats the topics, instruction and delight.

[64] S. H. Butcher in *Aristotle's Theory of Poetry and Fine Art*, London, 1895, p. 185.

[65] Lee, *op.cit.*, p. 227.

[66] From Castelvetro's *Poetica d'Aristotele* as translated by George Saintsbury in *A History of Criticism and Literary Taste in Europe*, London, 1902, II, p. 87.

[67] From a letter of Tasso; see *Lettere*, ii, 195. Quoted by J. E. Spingarn, *A History of Literary Criticism in the Renaissance*, 2d ed., New York, 1924, p. 55.

French translation of the *Dialogo*: "Il faut que vous sachiez que le peintre ne doit pas rechercher les louanges, et l'estime par une seule partie, mais par toutes celles qui concourent à la peinture, et sur tout par celles qui plaisent davantage. Si le peintre ne plait pas, il reste sans nom, et dans l'obscurité."[68]

On January 1, 1857, Delacroix recorded similar views of Poussin and Voltaire. He paraphrased Poussin's famous definition of art when he wrote, "Poussin définit le beau: la délectation."[69] In fact, Poussin's notably succinct definition had comprised more than a mere statement of the aim of painting, including as it did the traditional conception of the imitation of external reality: "C'est une imitation faites avec lignes et couleurs en quelque superficie de tout ce qui se voit dessous le soleil, sa fin est la délectation."[70] Although Delacroix recorded his paraphrase of Poussin's definition without further comment, he utilized the passage as a springboard for a discussion of beauty in which he disdains theories that define it as "regularity" or "the manifestation of good" in favor of one that derives from Voltaire's article on Aristotle. This one had asserted that "nous n'appelons *beau* que ce qui cause à notre âme et à nos sens du plaisir et de l'admiration."[71]

In view of the *caractère molochiste* of his art and his serious and profound conception of art as a bridge between the soul of the artist and that of the spectator, his insistence that art must please may come as a surprise. Yet we have discovered that he was aware of past theory that had justified the representation of scenes of terror and anguish in art. Furthermore, a passage from his writings makes it abundantly clear that he was vitally interested in the problem of the relation of art to moral didacticism.

In the *Œuvres littéraires* a long passage is devoted to a discus-

---

[68] Dolce, *Dialogue sur la peinture, intitulé l'Aretin*, p. 209. In Italian: "Bisogna, che voi sappiate, che'l Pittore non dee procacciar laude da una parte sola, ma da tutte quelle, che ricercano alla Pittura, e piu da quelle, che piu dilettano. Percioche essendo la Pittura trovata principalmente per dilettare, se'l Pittor non diletta se ne sta oscuro e senza nome." *Ibid.*, p. 208.

[69] *Journal*, III, p. 1 (January 1, 1857).

[70] See *Lettres de Poussin*, ed. Pierre du Colombier, Paris, 1929, p. 310. The letter, written to A. M. Chambray, is dated March 1, 1665, at Rome. An edition of Poussin's letters had appeared in 1824, compiled by Quatremère de Quincy and entitled *Collection de lettres de Nicolas Poussin*.

[71] *Journal*, III, p. 2 (January 1, 1857). For the source, see Voltaire, *Questions sur l'Encyclopédie par des amateurs*, I (deuxième partie), p. 110.

sion of this problem. Beginning with a citation of Kant's concept of the beautiful and the useful, it concludes with an allusion to the Germanic conception of ideal beauty. This is the passage that Lucien Rudrauf, Hubert Gillot, and René Huyghe cite as Delacroix's own in their interpretations of his conception of imitation.[72] The first paragraph begins: "Kant, en séparant le beau de l'utile, prouve clairement qu'il n'est point du tout dans la nature des arts de donner des leçons." It concludes with this ringing assertion: "L'on pourrait appliquer cette parole aux beaux-arts en général: ils doivent élever l'âme, et non pas l'endoctriner."[73] Actually, this is not Delacroix speaking at all for the entire passage is demonstrably a quotation, very precise and exact, from Madame de Staël's De l'Allemagne.[74]

Once the true authorship of this passage has been indicated, there remains to consider the significance of Delacroix's interest in it. In this respect it is well to recall the strong moralizing and didactic trend that had characterized the theory and practice of David and his school. David, in November 1793, had declared: "Les arts doivent donc puissamment contribuer à l'instruction publique. . . . C'est alors que les traits d'héroïsme, de vertus civiques, offerts aux regards du peuple électriseront son âme et feront germer en lui toutes les passions de la gloire, de dévouement pour sa patrie."[75] And, as late as 1827, his Death of Socrates of 1787 was described by a critic as "la gloire de la vertu et le triomphe de l'école française."[76]

Diderot, who provided a source for so many ideas congenial to Delacroix, in this context sounded a call to moral arms in painting — a position that Delacroix would have repudiated. "La peinture,"

[72] Lucien Rudrauf, Delacroix et le problème du romantisme artistique, p. 299; Hubert Gillot, E. Delacroix: l'homme, ses idées, son œuvre, p. 328; and R. Huyghe, Delacroix, p. 78.

[73] Œuvres littéraires, I, p. 65.

[74] Compare this passage with its source in De l'Allemagne, pp. 479-80. Hubert Gillot, op.cit., p. 328, also cites a portion of this quotation as the basis for a discussion of Delacroix's interpretation of nature.

[75] M. E. J. Delécluze, Louis David: son école et son temps, Paris, 1855, p. 158.

[76] Stamati Bulgari in Sur le but moral des arts, Paris, 1827, p. 2. Quoted by Léon Rosenthal, La peinture romantique, Paris, 1900, p. 12. Bulgari goes on to affirm that "l'estime et la considération dues à un artiste doivent être proportionnés au degré d'élévation de ses œuvres vers les convenances de la morale et de la perfection de l'art."

wrote Diderot, "a cela de commun avec la poésie, et il semble qu'on ne s'en soit pas encore avisé, que toutes deux elles doivent être *bene moratae*; il faut qu'elles aient des mœurs."[77] On the other hand, Voltaire, in his *Mélanges littéraires*, which Delacroix knew,[78] assumed a more drastically antimoralistic stand than Kant. With his customary probing cynicism he clearly mocked the traditional coupling of art and morality: "On se moquerait d'un homme qui demanderait si la fin de la peinture est d'instruire ou de plaire; il en est de même de la poésie; elle est indifférente au vice et à la vertu, et peut également servir l'un et l'autre."[79]

Delacroix, however much he admired Voltaire, never followed him in dissociating art and morality. Neither did he accept Diderot's didactic scheme. But we have seen that, by the very notation of a long passage from Madame de Staël, he was aware of and interested in the Kantian separation of art from the practical. His quotation of the de Staël excerpt is without any immediate comment but elsewhere, in the Journal entry of February 22, 1860, he suggests a subtle interpretation of the problem. Here, in the course of a discussion in which he shows some dissatisfaction with sheer *délectation* as the aim of art, he wonders whether the very order and arrangement of composition might not exert some moral persuasion: "N'y a-t-il pas, indépendamment de l'intérêt que l'esprit trouve dans la marche simple et claire d'une composition, dans le charme des situations habilement ménagées, une sorte de sens moral attaché même à une fable?"[80] In this assertion that aesthetic form possesses the power to exert a moral effect the influence of Madame de Staël is no doubt present. In *De l'Allemagne* (in the passage copied by Delacroix) she had indicated that, while Kant had properly denied the arts didactic powers, the phenomenon of beauty could, nevertheless, inspire virtue: "Sans doute, tout ce qui est beau doit faire naître des sentiments généreux, et

---

[77] Diderot, *Essais sur la peinture*, p. 83. Diderot thereafter gives his famous characterization of Boucher as "toujours vicieux" and Greuze as "toujours honnête."

[78] Delacroix who on August 1, 1860, had declared, "Je lis toujours *Voltaire* avec délices" (*Journal*, III, p. 302), quotes in the same entry a long passage from Voltaire's *Mélanges* concerning alleged deficiencies in Jean-Jacques Rousseau's style.

[79] *Œuvres complètes de Voltaire*, Paris, 1832, LXIII, p. 418.

[80] *Journal*, III, p. 267.

ces sentiments excitent à la vertu; mais, dès qu'on a pour objet de mettre en évidence un précepte de morale, la libre impression que produisent les chefs-d'œuvre de l'art est nécessairement détruite. . . ."[81]

THE PARAGONE

Another example of Delacroix's extraordinary involvement with the major themes of traditional art theory is evident in his many references to the *paragone,* the comparison of the arts, which, ever since Leonardo da Vinci's classic statement in his *Treatise on Painting,* had stimulated wide interest among art critics.[82] This theme was an especially congenial one because of his intense interest in all the arts. His own literary powers were prodigious and he freely exercised them not only in the private pages of the Journal but also, publicly, in the numerous articles now collected in the *Œuvres littéraires.* Many passages of the Journal testify to his ample knowledge and critical appreciation of music.[83] And his ability as a critic of sculpture appears in an article on Puget published in the *Plutarque français* in 1845.[84]

Another motivating factor in his treatment of the *paragone* recalls that which stimulated Leonardo's work: the exaltation of the art which he practiced most fluently as superior to all other arts. Delacroix never tired of emphasizing one factor which made painting superior to the temporal arts — its ability to register an effect

[81] De Staël, *op.cit.,* p. 479.

[82] For Leonardo's *paragone* and a valuable discussion of this conception, see *Paragone: A Comparison of the Arts by Leonardo da Vinci,* intro. and tr. Irma A. Richter, Oxford, 1949. For further ramifications of this idea in related areas of art theory, see Karl Borinski, *Die Antike in Poetik und Kunsttheorie,* 2 vols., Leipzig, 1914-24; Rensselaer W. Lee, "*Ut Pictura Poesis* . . . ," pp. 197-269; and Rémy G. Saisselin, "*Ut Pictura Poesis*: Dubos to Diderot," *Journal of Aesthetics and Art Criticism,* xx, no. 2 (Winter 1961), pp. 145-56. In somewhat modified form, my discussion of this subject appeared in my article, "*Ut Pictura Musica*: A Study of Delacroix's *Paragone,*" *Art Bulletin,* xlv (September 1963), pp. 266-71.

[83] See, for example, in the *Journal,* i, pp. 283-84 (April 7, 1849), the record of a recent conversation with Chopin on the subject of art and science (already cited, p. 12, n. 5) during which the relative merits of Mozart, Beethoven, and Berlioz were examined. Berlioz emerges poorly. In Delacroix's view, he merely "plaque des accords, et remplit comme il peut les intervalles." For the relationship between the painter and Chopin, see J. Starzynski, "Delacroix et Chopin," *Académie polonaise des sciences,* fascicule xxxiv, 1962, pp. 5-7.

[84] *Œuvres littéraires,* ii, pp. 105-23.

instantaneously — a characteristic already described by Leonardo and repeated ad infinitum in following centuries of art criticism.[85] Beethoven's *Pastoral Symphony* inspired him to remark, since he considered the length of the German master's works obnoxious, that "la peinture, entre autres avantages, a celui d'être plus discrète; le tableau le plus gigantesque se voit en un instant."[86] Leonardo had stated this idea in the following manner: "Painting makes an immediate presentation to you of the view which the artist has created. . . . Now see what a difference there is between hearing a thing related, which, over a period of time gives pleasure to the ear, and seeing it instantaneously with that speed with which things in nature are seen."[87]

This instantaneity of effect favored painting, in Delacroix's view, with an insuperable advantage over the temporal arts. For, from this quality derived its power to impress the spectator with the total burden of its intent immediately and as a whole whereas in literature, for example, the effect of the whole is necessarily vitiated, extended as it is over a period of time: "Vous voyez votre tableau d'un coup d'œil; dans votre manuscrit, vous ne voyez pas même la page entière, c'est-à-dire, vous ne pouvez pas l'embrasser tout entière par l'esprit."[88] Here again he is merely echoing the sentiments of Leonardo, who had stated: "The poet cannot give you in words the true shape of the parts of which the whole is composed, as can the painter, who places it before you with the same truthfulness that is in nature."[89] In Delacroix's conception, however, as we shall discover, there is no attempt to use this advantage to obtain mere fidelity to nature.

For the superiority of painting there remains one other argument that can be traced ultimately to Leonardesque origins — the superiority of the physical organ to which painting appeals. Delacroix, having recently observed some tapestries designed by Rubens which depicted the life of Achilles, compared the Flemish master favorably, indeed more than favorably, with Homer. And Rubens

---

[85] Franciscus Junius, Charles Lebrun, Félibien, de Piles, Dryden, Dubos, Lessing, Diderot, Voltaire, the Comte de Caylus, and Sir Joshua Reynolds, not to exhaust the list, all mention it as one of the proofs of the superiority of painting.
[86] *Journal*, I, p. 275 (March 11, 1849).
[87] Leonardo da Vinci, *Treatise on Painting*, I, p. 25.
[88] *Journal*, I, p. 393 (July 21, 1850).   [89] Leonardo da Vinci, *op.cit.*, I, p. 27.

deserved the palm precisely because his medium appealed to the superior sense of sight. "Voilà Homère et plus qu'Homère," he wrote, "car le poète ne me fait voir son Hector qu'avec les yeux de l'esprit, et ici je le vois avec ceux du corps. Ici est la grande supériorité de la peinture: à savoir, quand l'image offerte aux yeux non seulement satisfait l'imagination, mais encore fixe pour toujours l'objet et va au delà de la conception."[90]

This capacity of the painter, in representing the object to the physical eye, to fix that object concretely and forever, while the poet must remain content to appeal directly to the weaker image-retaining resources of the mind, had already been posed by Leonardo, who conceived of the eye as the noblest sense[91] and stated the case in words that clearly anticipate those of Delacroix: "Poetry places things before the imagination in words, while painting really places the objects before the eye, and the eye accepts the likenesses as though they were real."[92] Like many of Leonardo's ideas this conception entered the mainstream of art theory where it can be discerned in the work of de Piles, Du Fresnoy, Addison, Dubos, and Diderot. Diderot, moreover, knowingly pointed out that the notion of the superiority of sight had already appeared in the *Ars poetica* of Horace.[93]

In his conception of sight, Delacroix displays knowledge not only of theory inspired by the Antique and Renaissance past. More recent interpretations colored his thought and enabled him to regard this organ as the most efficient transmitter of Romantic con-

[90] *Journal*, I, p. 446 (January 27, 1852). Rubens' series of tapestries illustrating the life of Achilles had belonged to Louis-Philippe and was sold in 1852 at Monceaux; see Max Rooses, *L'Œuvre de P. P. Rubens*, Antwerp, 1890, III, p. 41.
[91] "That is more worthy which satisfies the better sense. Therefore, painting which satisfies the sense of sight is more noble than music, which satisfies only hearing." Leonardo da Vinci, *op.cit.*, I, pp. 14-15.
[92] *Ibid.*, p. 13.
[93] Diderot, in the *Essai sur la peinture* (p. 85), quotes these lines from the *Ars poetica*, v, 179:

> Segnus irritant animos dimissa per aurem,
> Quam quae sunt oculis subjecta fidelibus, et quae
> Ipse sibi tradit spectator?

Delacroix was a great admirer of Horace; in a letter of 1818 to his friend Félix Guillemardet, he declared, "Horace est à mon avis le plus grand médecin de l'âme, celui qui vous attache le mieux à la vie dans certaines circonstances, et qui vous apprend le plus à la mépriser dans d'autres." *Correspondance générale*, I, p. 31.

tent. For, unlike Leonardo, he did not conceive of painting as the means of mirroring the facts of visual nature. Painting was for him the most appropriate mode of artistic expression because of its ability to transmit intangible and subjective content — content impossible to characterize in words: "L'écrivain dit presque tout pour être compris. Dans la peinture il s'établi comme un pont mystérieux entre l'âme des personnages et celle du spectateur."[94]

Already in the early part of the eighteenth century writers had begun to regard sight as the purveyor of emotive and irrational impulses to the spectator. The Abbé Dubos, in *Réflexions critiques sur la poésie et sur la peinture*, proclaimed the superiority of sight, but, unlike Leonardo, because it possessed "plus d'empire sur l'âme que les autres sens."[95] Roger de Piles, in *Cours de peinture par principes*, claimed that sight constitutes "le sens le plus subtil, le plus capable de nous ébranler, et d'émouvoir nos passions."[96] And, later, Diderot, while comparing the manner in which poetry, painting, and music might treat the subject of a dying woman in his *Lettre sur les sourds et muets* of 1751, stressed the tangibility painting lent to the pathetic theme. "Le peintre," he indicated, "n'ayant qu'un moment, n'a pu rassembler autant de symptômes mortels que le poëte, mais en revanche ils sont bien plus frappants; c'est la chose même que le peintre montre. . . ."[97] Delacroix had only to refine this conception of the ability of painting to achieve a uniquely tangible response, declaring that "ce genre d'émotion propre à la peinture est *tangible* en quelque sorte; la poésie et la musique ne peuvent le donner. Vous jouissez de la représentation réelle de ces objets, comme si vous les voyiez véritablement, et en même temps le sens que renferment les images pour l'esprit vous échauffe et vous transporte."[98] In this characterization of painting as the art of rendering the intangible tangible he clearly formulated eighteenth-century intimations of this conception in a manner prophetic of later developments in painting.

---

[94] *Journal*, I, p. 17 (October 8, 1822).

[95] Dubos, *op.cit.*, I, p. 375. For Dubos' contribution to art theory, see A. Lombard, *L'Abbé Dubos: un initiateur de la pensée moderne*, Paris, 1913.

[96] De Piles, *Cours de peinture par principes*, p. 450.

[97] Denis Diderot, "Lettre sur les sourds et muets," *Œuvres complètes de Diderot*, I, pp. 387-88.

[98] *Journal*, II, p. 97 (October 17, 1853).

If painting was now to stress expression of intangible content as a major aim, music, not poetry or sculpture, became its most formidable rival among the arts. In this respect, Delacroix was but reflecting the new prestige of music as a nonmimetic and directly expressive medium. In the realm of literary theory a similar phenomenon occurred. As M. H. Abrams has put it: "In place of painting music becomes the art frequently pointed to as having a profound affinity with poetry."[99] As we shall discover, the most direct inspiration for Delacroix's comparison of painting and music was Madame de Staël. Their point of view, however, represents no new phenomenon, but rather the culmination of an ever-increasing interest in the analogy between the two arts which has its modern roots in the writings of the Renaissance.[100]

Leonardo's adherence to the mimetic function of art had led him to rank music far below painting. "Painting," he insisted, "is to be placed before all other activities because it contains all forms that are and those that are not to be found in nature, and it is more to be magnified and exalted than is music, which concerns only the voice."[101] At the same time, he voiced the theme of analogous harmony that would receive constant attention in later comparisons. For, unlike the musician and the painter, the poet "cannot describe the harmony of music, since he has not the power to say different

[99] M. H. Abrams, *The Mirror and the Lamp: Romantic Theory and the Critical Tradition*, New York, 1953, p. 50.

[100] For the growing importance of music in the comparison of the arts, see especially: F. Baldensperger, *Sensibilité musicale et romantisme*, Paris, 1925; John W. Draper, "Poetry and Music in Eighteenth Century Aesthetics," *Englische Studien*, 1932, pp. 70-85; Herbert M. Schueller, "Literature and Music as Sister Arts: an Aspect of Aesthetic Theory in Eighteenth Century Britain," *Philological Quarterly*, XXVI, 1947, pp. 193-205, and "Correspondences between Music and the Sister Arts according to Eighteenth Century Theory," *Journal of Aesthetics and Art Criticism*, XI, 1953, pp. 334-59; Paul O. Kristeller, "The Modern System of the Arts: a Study of the History of Aesthetics," *Journal of the History of Ideas*, XII, 1951, pp. 496-527, and *ibid.*, XIII, 1952, pp. 17-46. On Delacroix and music, see especially G. J. Aubry, "Delacroix et la musique," *Revue musicale*, April 1, 1920; R. L. Evans, *Les romantiques françois et la musique*, Paris, 1934; J.-L. Vaudoyer, "Chopin et son ami Eugène Delacroix," *Revue française*, no. 18, 1948; M. H. Abrams, *op.cit.*, pp. 88-94; René Huyghe, "Delacroix and Baudelaire: A New Epoch in Art and Poetry," *Arts Yearbook 2*, 1958, pp. 27-46, and *Delacroix*, esp. pp. 193-98; and José Bruyr, "Delacroix et la musique," *Europe: revue mensuelle*, April 1963, pp. 97-99.

[101] Leonardo da Vinci, *op.cit.*, I, p. 15. For other Renaissance comparisons of music and painting, see Robert J. Clements, *Michelangelo's Theory of Art*, New York, 1961, pp. 52-55.

things at one time. The harmonious proportion of painting, composed of different parts at one time, does have this power, and its sweetness is judged simultaneously as a whole and in detail."[102] Harmony, be it of various parts or of the whole, became one of the major qualities shared by painting and music as described by writers such as Bellori, de Piles, Diderot and Baudelaire.[103] More pertinent to the matter at hand, however, is the emergence of an analogy of the two arts which emphasized their power to express the difficult, uncharted, inner world of feelings and emotions.

In his famous letter to his friend Chantelou concerning the "modes," Poussin had investigated the manner in which transformations of the analogous elements of music and painting determined contrasting expressive effects.[104] As Félibien described it, "il s'étoit imaginé que comme dans la Musique l'oreille ne se trouve charmée que par un juste accord de diférentes voix; de même dans la Peinture la vûë n'est agréablement satisfaite que par la

[102] Leonardo da Vinci, *op.cit.*, I, p. 27.

[103] Bellori, in his description of Giovanni Lanfranco's cupola at S. Andrea della Valle in Rome, wrote as follows: "Wherefore this painting has been compared rightly to full-bodied music, when all the tones together form a harmony . . ." Giovanni Pietro Bellori, *Le vite dei pittori, scultori ed architetti moderni*, Pisa, 1821, II, p. 111. (1st ed., 1672.)

De Piles: "Tous les objets visibles n'entrent dans l'esprit que par les organes des yeux, comme les sons dans la musique n'entrent dans l'esprit que par les oreilles. Les oreilles et les yeux sont les portes par lesquelles entrent nos jugemens sur les concerts de musique et sur les ouvrages de Peinture. Le premier soin du Peintre aussi-bien que du Musicien, doit donc être de rendre l'entrée de ces portes libre et agréable par la force de leur harmonie, l'un dans le Coloris accompagné de son Clair-obscur, et l'autre dans ses accords." De Piles, *op.cit.*, p. 9.

Diderot: "Il en est de la peinture, ainsi que de la musique; vous possédez les règles de la composition; vous connaissez tous les accords et leurs renversemens; les modulations s'enchaînent à votre gré sous vos doigts; vous avez l'art de lier, de rapprocher les cordes les plus disparates; vous produisez, quand il vous plaît, les effets d'harmonie les plus rares et les plus piquants." Diderot, "Salon de 1767," *Œuvres complètes*, XI, p. 312.

Baudelaire, in his review of the *Exposition universelle* of 1855, thus described the musical qualities of Delacroix's paintings: "Puis ces admirables accords de sa couleur font souvent rêver d'harmonie et de mélodie, et l'impression qu'on emporte de ses tableaux est souvent quasi musicale." Baudelaire, *Curiosités esthétiques* . . . , p. 238. Maxime du Camp, in his *Souvenirs littéraires* of 1882, was another early admirer of this quality in Delacroix's art: "C'est un procédé musical; aussi faisait-il des symphonies plutôt que des tableaux: l'*Entrée des Croisés à Constantinople* est une symphonie en bleu majeur, tandis que la *Barque des Naufragés* est une symphonie en vert mineur avec un rouge à la clef . . ." *Souvenirs littéraires de Maxime du Camp, 1822-1894*, introduction by Henri Lemaitre, Paris, 1962, pp. 269-70.

[104] See *Lettres de Poussin*, ed. Pierre du Colombier, pp. 238-43.

belle harmonie des couleurs, et la juste convenance de toutes les parties les unes auprès des autres. De sorte que considérant que la diférence des sons cause à l'âme des mouvemens diférens, selon qu'elle est touchée par des tons graves ou aigus, il ne doutoit pas que la manière d'exposer les objets dans une disposition de mouvemens, et une apparence d'expressions plus ou moins violentes, et sous des couleurs mises les unes auprès des autres et mélangées diversement, ne donnât à la vûë diverses sensations qui pouvoient rendre l'âme susceptible d'autant de passions diférentes."[105] According to Anthony Blunt, Poussin's ideas were culled almost word for word from the sixteenth-century treatise on music, *L'Istitutioni harmoniche*, by the Venetian writer, Gioseffo Zarlino (1517-90).[106] Nevertheless, Poussin evidenced thereby the growing preoccupation with this equation. In 1692, Charles Perrault, in his *Parallèle des anciens et des modernes en ce qui regarde les arts et les sciences*, declared that, just as in painting, one discovers that "dans la Musique le beau son et la justesse de la voix charment l'oreille, les mouvemens gais ou languissans de cette mesme voix selon les différentes passions qu'ils expriment, touchent le cœur. . . ."[107]

In the eighteenth century, writers began to focus their attention upon the central issue of the problem: the relation of music and painting to the new aim of the arts. As their vision gradually turned from the outer world to the inner world of man, the imitative aims and faculties of the arts became the core of the discussion. It is well to note that, in the beginning, there was no doubt that music, like painting and poetry, was essentially imitative in nature. Dubos, who was much concerned with the nature of music, paraphrased Aristotle's comparison of music and painting: "C'est ainsi qu'Aristote dit que la musique fait son imitation avec les tons, l'harmonie et le rithme, comme le Peintre fait son imitation avec

---

[105] André Félibien, *Conférences de l'académie royale de peinture et de sculpture*, pp. 22-23 (Preface).

[106] Anthony Blunt, "Poussin's Notes on Painting," *Journal of the Warburg Institute*, I, 1938, pp. 344-51. Also see the paraphrase of Blunt's Cambridge dissertation in Paul Alfassa, "L'Origine de la lettre de Poussin sur les modes d'après un travail récent," *Bulletin de la société de l'histoire de l'art français*, 1933, pp. 125-43.

[107] Charles Perrault, *Paralèlle [sic] des anciens et des modernes en ce qui regarde les arts et les sciences*, 2d ed., Paris, 1692, I, p. 214. (1st ed., 1688.)

les traits et les couleurs."[108] On this subject, Jean-Jacques Rousseau, a composer of note himself,[109] stressed the value of music as imitative of the new, subjective content of art: "C'est un des plus grands avantages du musicien, de pouvoir peindre les choses qu'on ne sauroit entendre, tandis qu'il est impossible au peintre de représenter celles qu'on ne sauroit voir . . . il ne représentera pas directement ces choses, mais il excitera dans l'âme les mêmes sentiments qu'on éprouve en les voyant."[110] It is worth noting, however, that he still conceived of painting as the rendering of things visible, thus retaining the Renaissance scheme.

Among English theoreticians who advocated the emotional and intangible as the special province of music was James Harris, who, in his *Discourse on Music, Painting, and Poetry* of 1744, described the power of music as one "which consists not in Imitations, and the raising *Ideas*; but in raising Affections, to which Ideas may correspond."[111] At the same time, he too regarded painting as "the Media of *visible* objects."[112] Later, Sir Joshua Reynolds, in his thirteenth *Discourse* of December 11, 1786, noted the power of music to present its content to the imagination without the intervention of "real" subject matter including architecture, and even poetry, among those arts which shared this faculty: "It [architecture] applies itself, like Musick (and I believe we may add Poetry) directly to the imagination, without the intervention of any kind of imitation."[113]

In France, this conception had already appeared in the writings of Diderot, who, in May 1751, posed the following question in a letter to a friend: "Comment se fait-il donc que, des trois arts imi-

[108] Dubos, *op.cit.*, I, p. 416. For Aristotle's comparison, see *The Poetics of Aristotle*, ed. and tr. S. H. Butcher, p. 7. "For as there are persons who, by conscious art or mere habit, imitate and represent various objects through the medium of colour and form, or again by the voice; so in the arts above mentioned [epic poetry, tragedy, comedy, dithyrambic poetry and music], taken as a whole, the imitation is produced by rhythm, language and 'harmony,' either singly or combined."

[109] For Rousseau's musical career, see Albert Jansen, *Jean-Jacques Rousseau als Musiker*, Berlin, 1884.

[110] Jean-Jacques Rousseau, "Essai sur l'origine des langues," *Œuvres complètes de J. J. Rousseau*, Paris, 1832, II, p. 377.

[111] James Harris, "A Discourse on Music, Painting, and Poetry," *Miscellanies by James Harris*, London, 1792, I, p. 99.

[112] *Ibid.*, p. 57.

[113] *Sir Joshua Reynolds: Discourses on Art*, p. 241.

tateurs de la nature, celui dont l'expression est la plus arbitraire et la moins précise parle le plus fortement à l'âme? Seroit-ce que, montrant moins les objets, il laisse plus de carrière à notre imagination; ou qu'ayant besoin de secousses pour être émus, la Musique est plus propre que la Peintre et la Poësie à produire en nous cet effet tumultueux?"[114]

It was in Germany, however, during the latter part of the eighteenth century and the early part of the nineteenth, that the exaltation of music as the Romantic art par excellence — the art which all others should emulate — became a prevailing point of view. Wilhelm Heinrich Wackenroder, in his *Phantasien über die Kunst für Freunde der Kunst* of 1799, which amounts to an ardent argument for the superiority of music over the other arts, claimed that "in the mirror of sounds the human heart recognizes itself; they are the means by which we learn to become sensitive to feeling; they endow many dreaming spirits in the hidden corners of the soul with a living consciousness and enrich our innermost being with completely new and magical spirits of feeling."[115] And, in 1795, Schiller, anticipating Pater, urged the visual arts to emulate the condition of music. "Plastic art in its highest consummation," he declared, "must become music, and move us by its direct sensuous presence."[116]

The chief avenue by which Delacroix became familiar with these German formulations of the nature of music and the arts was, of course, Madame de Staël.[117] This is evident in the passage that follows his acknowledgment of her contribution to his aesthetic. "Cet art [painting]," he continued, "ainsi que la musique, *sont au-dessus de la pensée*; de là leur avantage sur la littérature, par le vague."[118] Painting, like music, is superior to literature (and he underlines these words) because it is above thought. In the passage from *De l'Allemagne* which served as the source of this paraphrase, Madame de Staël had been even more precise and explicit in her description

---

[114] Denis Diderot, *Correspondance*, ed. Georges Roth, Paris, 1955, I, p. 128.

[115] Wilhelm Heinrich Wackenroder, "Phantasien über die Kunst für Freunde der Kunst," *Werke und Briefe*, Jena, 1910, I, p. 189.

[116] Johann Cristoph Friedrich von Schiller, "Upon the Aesthetic Culture of Man, in a Series of Letters," *The Philosophical and Aesthetic Letters and Essays of Schiller*, tr. J. Weiss, London, 1845, p. 135.

[117] See *Journal*, I, p. 50 (January 26, 1824).

[118] *Ibid.*

of the manner in which painting, like music, might express verbally inexpressible content: "Il y a de la pensée dans cette manière de concevoir les arts, comme dans les combinaisons ingénieuses de Gluck; mais les arts sont au-dessus de la pensée; leur langage, ce sont des couleurs, ou les formes ou les sons. Si l'on pouvait se figurer les impressions dont notre âme serait susceptible avant qu'elle connût la parole, on concevrait mieux l'effet de la peinture et de la musique."[119]

One discovers the conception of music as a prime medium for the expression of Romantic content again in Delacroix's writings — imbedded in that passage which he excerpted from *De l'Allemagne*,[120] a passage which concludes with this now familiar note: "L'homme a dans son âme des sentiments innés, que les objets réels ne satisferont jamais, et c'est à ces sentiments que l'imagination du peintre et du poète sait donner une forme et une vie. Le premier des arts, la musique, qu'imite-il?"[121]

While Delacroix revealed sympathy for the German admiration for music, he nevertheless favored painting over music as a Romantic medium. Music, he suggested, might very well be inferior in this respect since painting in its appeal to the sense of sight renders intangible content more tangible: "L'art du peintre est d'autant plus intime au cœur de l'homme qu'il paraît plus matériel; car chez lui, comme dans la nature extérieure, la part est faite franchement à ce qui est fini et à ce qui est infini, c'est-à-dire à ce que l'âme trouve qui la remue intérieurement dans les objets qui ne frappent que les sens."[122] In so doing, he thus linked two aspects of the *paragone*: the superiority of sight as the receptacle of concrete images — an argument originating in Antiquity, championed by Leonardo, and still present in Diderot; and painting and music as the arts of intangible, subjective expression, an idea of more recent vintage, evolving especially in the eighteenth century and available to him ascertainably via the writings of Madame de Staël. His awareness of the new orientation of the arts was indeed prophetic. One need only consult the writings of Whistler, Redon, Gauguin,

[119] De Staël, *op.cit.*, p. 407.
[120] See p. 19 and n. 19.
[121] *Œuvres littéraires*, I, p. 65.
[122] *Journal*, I, pp. 17-18 (October 8, 1822).

Matisse, and Kandinsky, among others, in order to realize how fundamental the analogy between painting and music was to become.[123]

Of sculpture, an erstwhile rival of painting as the supreme art, especially during the Renaissance, he had less to say. He was, however, well acquainted with the lively discussions the comparison of painting and sculpture had stimulated in the past. In his article on Michelangelo for the *Revue de Paris* of 1830 he noted that "on s'occupa pendant plus de cent ans de la question de la prééminence de la sculpture ou de la peinture. On n'imagine point tout ce qui fut écrit à ce sujet."[124] Furthermore, he cites, rather incredulously, what he considered the "singulier raisonnement" of Benvenuto Cellini, who had claimed superiority for the art of sculpture since it was "sept fois plus distinguée que la peinture, par la raison qu'il y a dans une statue sept points différents sous lesquels il faut que l'œil la trouve également correcte."[125] It is to be regretted that this

[123] Whistler claimed that "as music is the poetry of sound so is painting the poetry of sight, and the subject-matter has nothing to do with harmony of sound or of color." Quoted by Robert Goldwater and Marco Treves, *Artists on Art*, New York, 1945, p. 347. Redon wrote to a friend that his drawings "are not to be defined. They determine nothing. They place us, as does music, in the ambiguous realm of the undetermined. They are a kind of metaphor . . . ," *ibid.*, pp. 360-61; Gauguin insisted that "in painting one must search rather for suggestion than for description, as is done in music. Sometimes people accuse me of being incomprehensible only because they look for an explicative side to my pictures which is not there." *Ibid.*, p. 369. (See H. R. Rookmaker, *Synthetist Art Theories*, Amsterdam, 1959, pp. 210-20, for the growing importance of this analogy in nineteenth-century theory culminating in the ideas of Gauguin and his circle.) On the subject of imitation, Matisse wrote: "I cannot copy nature in a servile way, I must interpret nature and submit it to the spirit of the picture — when I have found the relationship of all the tones the result must be a living harmony of tones, a harmony not unlike that of a musical composition." Goldwater and Treves, *op.cit.*, p. 411. And, in 1912, Kandinsky made this analogy one of the leading themes of his argument in *Concerning the Spiritual in Art*, New York, 1947, p. 40: "A painter who finds no satisfaction in mere representation, however artistic, in his longing to express his internal life, cannot but envy the ease with which music, the least material of the arts today, achieves this end. He naturally seeks to apply the means of music to his own art."

[124] *Œuvres littéraires*, II, p. 53.

[125] Cellini's argument is to be found in his letter of January 28, 1546, written in response to Benedetto Varchi's questionnaire on the *paragone* sent to various artists including Pontormo, Bronzino, Vasari, and others. See Varchi's *Due lezioni sopra la pittura e scultura*, Florence, 1549. A French edition of the *Lettere pittoriche di Bottari e Ticozzi* of 1754, which has Cellini's letter, appeared in Paris in 1817: *Recueil de lettres sur la peinture, la sculpture et l'architecture*, tr. L.-J. Jay, Paris, 1817. From the letter as it appears in Jay's translation (p. 103), I quote Cellini's words: "Je dis que l'art de la sculpture,

acknowledgment of the existence of the traditional comparison of the two arts failed to inspire any comment or discussion beyond the irony inherent in the phrase, "singulier raisonnement." Sculpture, like painting, however, always remained one of Delacroix's preferred "silent arts": "L'ouvrage du peintre et du sculpteur est tout d'une pièce comme les ouvrages de la nature. L'auteur n'y est point présent, et n'est point en commerce avec vous comme l'écrivain ou l'orateur."[126] While acknowledging that painting and sculpture are "tout d'une pièce comme les ouvrages de la nature," he nowhere mentions the oft-repeated argument for the superiority of painting over sculpture as due to its ability to depict a far wider scope of naturalistic subject matter. Inspired by Leonardo's conception of painting as the imitation of nature, this notion achieved wide currency during the sixteenth century. Giorgio Vasari, for example, in his reply to Varchi's questionnaire, catalogued at some length the natural phenomena imitable by painting but impossible, or at least awkward, in sculpture. Painting, unlike sculpture, he suggests, "contrefait et imite parfaitment le souffle, l'eau, les vents, les tempêtes, la pluie, les nuages, la grêle, la neige, la glace, la foudre, les éclairs, la nuit, le crépuscule, le clair de la lune, le brillant des étoiles, les diverses espèces d'air pur ou chargé de vapeurs, l'ardeur plus ou moins grande de la chaleur du soleil ou du feu, les degrés forts ou faibles des lumières naturelles ou artificielles, enfin le soleil lui-même et sa splendeur."[127] Delacroix's silence re-

---

parmi tous les autres dans lesquels le dessin est nécessaire, est sept fois plus grand, parce qu'une statue doit avoir sept manières d'être vue. . . ." It is interesting to note that Michelangelo's comparison of painting and sculpture, which was included in his reply to Varchi's questionnaire, was also known to Delacroix. In the *Journal*, ii, p. 248 (August 31, 1854), Delacroix remarks that "il [Michelangelo] disait que la *bonne sculpture* était celle qui *ne ressemblait pas à la peinture*, et que la *bonne peinture*, au contraire, était celle qui *ressemblait à de la sculpture*." (Italics are Delacroix's.) Michelangelo, in Jay's translation, had written: "Je dis donc qu'une peinture me paraît être d'autant plus estimable, qu'elle approche davantage du relief, et que le relief est regardé d'autant plus mauvais, qu'il s'approche davantage de la peinture." *Recueil de lettres sur la peinture, la sculpture et l'architecture*, p. 133. This exchange between Varchi and Michelangelo was brought to Delacroix's attention by his friend, the eccentric painter and philosopher, Paul Chenavard. For the relationship between Delacroix and Chenavard see Joseph C. Sloane, *Paul Marc Joseph Chenavard: Artist of 1848*, Chapel Hill, 1962, esp. pp. 164-68.

126 *Journal*, ii, p. 276 (September 23, 1854).
127 From Vasari's letter as rendered by Jay, *op.cit.*, p. 109.

garding this obvious attribute of his medium derives, no doubt, from his strong bias against the Realists, who would probably have given enthusiastic approval to Vasari's argument.

In his treatment of the *paragone*, which exploits ideas that can be traced back to Leonardo da Vinci as well as more recent sources in German thought as popularized by Madame de Staël, Delacroix reveals with striking clarity the strong links that bind him to the art theory of the past. As we have discovered, this is true, as well, of other aspects of his conception of art. With so much evidence established for his extraordinary commitment to antecedent art theory, we may now turn to the analysis of his treatment of an aspect of aesthetic theory which, from its very beginnings, assumed eminence as the central topic of all theoretical inquiry — the problem of imitation.

IMITATION

IF ART IS to be defined as a bridge between the soul of the artist and the soul of the spectator, the nature of the bridge requires further, rather special elucidation. The inevitable questions which have plagued art theorists of all periods and which demand extraordinarily delicate solutions in a Romantic context immediately arise: To what extent should the painter in his quest to embody his inner life rely upon the depiction of visual reality? To what extent should he depend upon previous stylistic formulas as aids to expression? Delacroix was characteristically articulate on these matters and his position regarding the imitation of nature and the imitation of the Antique can be easily charted. As always, his ideas reflect, directly and indirectly, his awareness of antecedent solutions to these problems.

THE IMITATION OF NATURE

When Delacroix expressed his distaste for works of the Realist persuasion,[1] his opposition did not rest merely on gentlemanly dismay in the face of vulgar subject matter. Rather, it was symbolic of his deep preoccupation with the whole problem of imitation. In his view, literal transcription of the facts of nature only hin-

---

[1] Recall his unhappy reaction to Courbet's *Bathers* (see above p. 18 and n. 23). See also the entry in the Journal of February 22, 1860, which contains a long discussion of the nature of Realism; here he suggests that "le réalisme devrait être défini l'antipode de l'art. Il est peut-être plus odieux dans la peinture et dans la sculpture que dans l'histoire et le roman . . ." *Journal*, III, p. 266. Even in the novel he had little patience with the style; in reference to Balzac's *Ursule Mirouet*, he wrote: "J'ai pris *Ursule Mirouet*, de Balzac; toujours ces tableaux d'après des pygmées dont il montre tous les détails, que le personnage soit le principal ou seulement un personnage accessoire. Malgré l'opinion surfaite du mérite de Balzac, je persiste à trouver son genre faux d'abord et faux ensuite ses caractères." *Journal*, III, p. 300 (July 22, 1860).

dered the artist's attempt to render an adequate representation of reality since "plus elle est littérale, cette imitation, plus elle est plate, plus elle montre combien toute rivalité est impossible. On ne peut espérer d'arriver qu'à des équivalents."[2]

On the other hand, he clearly dissociated himself from what he considered Mannerist tendencies of the day, especially as fostered by Academic emphasis on the repetition of formulas derived from old masters, a method he denounced as "ce point qui sera toujours le mot d'ordre de toutes les écoles: imiter le technique de cette école-ci ou de cette école-là . . . copier l'exécution du Guide ou celle de Raphaël, suivant la mode."[3] The irony inherent in this passage no doubt applied in his mind to his arch-rival, Ingres, whose works had shared a place of honor with his at the *Exposition Universelle* of 1855. On this very occasion he expressed a fundamental aversion to Ingres' exhibit, declaring that "le ridicule, dans cette exhibition, domine à un grand degré; c'est l'expression complète d'une incomplète intelligence; l'effort et la prétention sont partout; il ne s'y trouve pas une étincelle de naturel."[4]

With the rejection of these two extremes Delacroix faced the task of charting a satisfactory course between the Realist Scylla of Courbet and the Mannerist Charybdis of Ingres. It will be our endeavor to follow his rather devious course, noting, along the way, his reliance upon previous landmarks.

One might well begin by inquiring why it was that he opposed so vigorously an art that claimed complete allegiance to visual reality — why, in his view, objective and unadorned transcription of the facts of nature failed to qualify as suitable material for artistic representation. In part, the answer lies in his ambivalent attitude toward nature. On October 12, 1853, he recorded in the Journal a passage that sets forth a philosophy of nature in which the inner life of the individual takes precedence over the ephemeral and transitory reality offered by the objective world of visual fact. "Il est donc beaucoup plus important pour l'artiste de se rapprocher de l'idéal qu'il porte en lui, et qui lui est particulier, que de laisser, même avec force, l'idéal passager que peut présenter la na-

---

[2] *Journal*, II, p. 192 (May 25, 1854).
[3] *Journal*, II, p. 414 (November 25, 1855).
[4] *Journal*, II, p. 327 (May 15, 1855).

ture. . . ."[5] Therefore, since nature carries in itself but a transitory ideal, one of no permanent value, the artist must seek one within himself and the image of nature must be subordinated to whatever this interior image might impose upon it.

This constitutes, of course, a complete reversal of the ubiquitous ideal of exact imitation of nature announced, in the Renaissance, by Alberti,[6] recapitulated and developed by Leonardo,[7] and repeated throughout the sixteenth century by Lodovico Dolce, Giorgio Vasari, and others.[8] Furthermore, in Delacroix's comprehensive picture of the rise and fall of styles in art, exact imitation of nature occurred primarily during periods of qualitative decadence. "C'est ordinairement dans les époques de décadence qu'on a vu attacher plus de prix à la perfection de l'imitation."[9]

[5] *Journal*, II, p. 87 (October 12, 1853). This is an excerpt from a long passage entitled "De l'emploi du modèle," which has many significant statements concerning imitation.

[6] "No one would deny that the painter has nothing to do with things that are not visible. The painter is concerned solely with representing what can be seen." Alberti, *On Painting*, p. 43.

[7] "That painting is most praiseworthy which conforms most to the object portrayed." Leonardo da Vinci, *Treatise on Painting*, I, p. 161. In view of Delacroix's expressed desire to write a commentary on Leonardo's treatise, it is worth noting that Leonardo, unlike Delacroix, based the superiority of painting over poetry, in part, on its fidelity to nature: "Painting presents the works of nature to the senses with more truth and certainty than do words or letters. But letters present words with greater truth than does painting. Let us state that science to be more admirable which represents the works of nature, than that which represents the works of workers, that is, the works of men." *Ibid.*, p. 9.

[8] For the development of the conception of imitation in the Renaissance and Baroque periods, see Lee, "*Ut Pictura Poesis* . . . ," pp. 203-10.

[9] *Journal*, III, p. 361 (Supplément). On this matter, he elsewhere suggested that "les arts ont leur enfance, leur virilité et leur décrépitude. Il y a des génies vigoureux qui sont venus trop tôt, de même qu'il y en a qui viennent trop tard; dans les uns et les autres, on trouve des saillies singulières. Les talents primitifs n'arrivent pas plus à la perfection que les talents des temps de la décadence." *Journal*, I, p. 343 (February 19, 1850). In view of his distaste for the Realists and Academics of his own day, it is not unlikely that he conceived of himself as one of those "génies vigoureux" who were born too late and in a period of decadence. This would correspond very nicely with his general pessimism regarding philosophies of social and cultural progress. Furthermore, it would enhance the Romantic image of himself as an artist-hero battling current tides of vulgarity and degeneration of taste. He considered Mozart and Cimarosa to have lived in congenial times for artistic expression while Rossini and Beethoven, more nearly his contemporaries, proved unable, despite genius, to rise above the "mannerism" of their period: "Du temps de Mozart et de Cimarosa, on compterait quarante musiciens qui semblent être de leur famille, et dont les ouvrages contiennent, à des degrés différents, toutes les conditions de la perfection. A partir de ce moment, tout le génie des Rossini et des Beethoven ne peut

The negative attitude toward nature so positively expressed in these passages provided a firm foundation for the withering criticism he directed at the Realist school. Speaking generally of this movement, he declared: "La plupart de ces peintres, qui sont si scrupuleux dans l'emploi du modèle, n'exercent la plupart du temps leur talent de le copier avec fidélité que sur des compositions mal digérées et sans intérêt. Ils croient avoir tout fait, quand ils ont reproduit des têtes, des mains, des accessoires imités servilement et sans rapport mutuel."[10]

Here it should be recalled that, even during the height of Renaissance interest in the faithful transcription of nature, there had existed, quite concurrently, the contrary idea that nature must be generalized and embellished.[11] Of course, Ancient theory had already posed the same seeming paradox[12] while, in the post-Renaissance, the conception of a typical and embellished nature was to flourish — especially as "la belle nature" adopted by French Classical doctrine soon after it had been formulated in Italy by Giovanni Bellori.[13]

It was during the eighteenth century, however, that the authority of the conception of exact imitation was seriously questioned. Already in 1699 Roger de Piles had declared that "un habile Peintre ne doit point être esclave de la Nature, il en doit être Arbitre, et judicieux imitateur. . . ."[14] In 1719, Jean Baptiste Dubos more

---

les sauver de la *manière*. C'est par la manière qu'on plaît à un public blasé et avide par conséquent de nouveautés; c'est aussi la manière qui fait vieillir promptement les ouvrages de ces artistes inspirés, mais dupes eux-mêmes de cette fausse nouveauté qu'ils ont cru introduire dans l'art." *Ibid.*, p. 343.

[10] *Journal*, II, p. 88 (October 12, 1853).

[11] Alberti had already described the painter's task as more than the mere transcription of visual reality: "It will please him not only to make all the parts true to his model but also to add beauty there; because in painting, liveliness is not less pleasing than richness." Alberti, *On Painting*, p. 92.

[12] As Panofsky puts it: "In Antiquity, thought in respect to the arts had from the beginning juxtaposed with complete ingenuousness (as the Renaissance would later) two contrary ideas: the idea that art is inferior to nature in so far as it merely imitates nature, at best to the point of deception — and the idea that the work of art is superior to nature in so far as, by compensating for the imperfection of her individual productions, it confronts her with an independently created image of beauty." Erwin Panofsky, *Idea: ein Beitrag zur Begriffsgeschichte der älteren Kunsttheorie*, Berlin, 1960, p. 7.

[13] For the development of the concept of "la belle nature" see Lee's discussion of Imitation in "*Ut Pictura Poesis* . . . ," pp. 203-10.

[14] Roger de Piles, *Dialogue sur le coloris*, Paris, 1699, p. 8.

drastically relegated imitation of nature to a secondary role, claiming that "il faut sçavoir faire quelque chose de plus que copier servilement la nature, pour donner à chaque passion son caractère convenable, et pour bien exprimer les sentiments de tous les personnages d'un tableau. Il faut, pour ainsi dire, sçavoir copier la nature sans la voir."[15] Thereafter, especially in Germany, there was forged a new aesthetic which exalted art as the mirror of the artist's "soul" so that by 1810 Madame de Staël was able to supply to Delacroix, in the passage quoted by him in the *Œuvres littéraires*, a coherent and persuasive statement of this position: "Les Allemands ne considèrent point, ainsi qu'on le fait d'ordinaire, l'imitation de la nature comme le principal objet de l'art; c'est la beauté idéale qui leur paraît le principe de tous les chefs-d'œuvre, et leur théorie poétique est, à cet égard, tout à fait d'accord avec leur philosophie. L'impression qu'on reçoit par les beaux-arts n'a pas le moindre rapport avec le plaisir que fait éprouver une imitation quelconque; l'homme a dans son âme des sentiments innés que les objets réels ne satisferont jamais, et c'est à ces sentiments que l'imagination des peintres et des poëtes sait donner une forme et une vie. Le premier des arts, la musique, qu'imite-t-il?"[16]

Delacroix's attitude towards exact imitation of nature found its way into precepts imparted to Louis de Planet, his pupil and assistant in the decoration of the Library of the Palais Bourbon. In his *Souvenirs*, a recollection of association with the master which furnishes significant clues to the nature of Delacroix's ideas from 1838 to 1844 — years for which no Journals exist — Planet cites many examples of his mentor's position on this subject. On one occasion, Delacroix pointed out that "le modèle vivant . . . ne rend jamais exactement l'idée de la figure qu'on veut représenter: il est ou mesquin, ou incomplet, ou d'une beauté tellement différente et supérieure qu'on est amené à tout changer. . . ."[17] Another example of this lack of commitment to the faithful representation of visual fact occurred on November 17, 1841, when, faced with the problem of depicting palm trees, Planet received advice that a Realist would

[15] Dubos, *Réflexions critiques sur la poésie et sur la peinture*, I, p. 200.
[16] See Madame de Staël, *De l'Allemagne*, p. 480; in Delacroix, this passage is quoted in the *Œuvres littéraires*, I, pp. 66-67.
[17] Louis de Planet, *Souvenirs de travaux de peinture avec M. Eugène Delacroix*, ed. A. Joubin, Paris, 1929, p. 35; from a passage dated November 3, 1841.

have abhorred: "Comme il n'avait pas de modèles, M. Delacroix m'a donné un pot de fleurs, un œillet dont les tiges élancées et les feuilles allongées et divergentes pouvaient m'être utiles, quoique différentes de celles du palmier. *Tout ce qui, dans la nature, se rapproche de l'objet à représenter, sert en l'absence du véritable modèle.*"[18] This frank willingness, underscored by Planet, to utilize substitutes for natural phenomena recalls the procedure of certain Renaissance and Baroque artists[19] and almost reverts to the medieval principle enunciated by Cennino Cennini when he advised his reader in the proper manner of drawing a mountain: "If you wish to draw mountains well, so that they appear natural, procure some large stones, rocky and not polished, and draw from these, giving them lights and shades as the same rule guides you."[20]

Moreover, Planet tells us that Delacroix considered the intervention of nature, once the creative process had begun, a major blunder in the production of a truly vital work of art, citing the working procedures of Titian and Rubens. "Il [Delacroix] considère extrêmement funeste l'habitude de se servir du modèle; c'est cela qui avait conduit Titien à refroidir un peu le mouvement de ses figures. Titien ébauchait son tableau d'inspiration; puis il le reprenait morceau par morceau, d'après nature. . . ."[21] Rubens, who reversed this process and added individual embellishment to an initial sketch after nature, demonstrated the preferred way: "Au contraire, Rubens ne faisait que le croquis d'après nature; il peignait ensuite d'inspiration, dégagé du modèle."[22] Nature, suspect as the unadorned subject matter of the Romantic painter, is thus relegated to a secondary position during the organic development of the work of art.

[18] *Ibid.*, p. 53; from a passage dated November 17, 1841. It was Planet's habit to underline especially memorable advice from his master.

[19] For example, Poussin, who, in Félibien's words, "disposait sur une table de petits modèles qu'il couvrait de vêtements pour juger de l'effet et de la disposition de tous les corps ensemble, et cherchait si fort à imiter toujours la nature, que je l'ai vu considérer jusqu'à des pierres, à des mottes de terre, et à des morceaux de bois, pour mieux imiter des rochers, des terrasses, et des troncs d'arbres." André Félibien, *Entretiens sur la vie et les ouvrages de Nicolas Poussin*, Geneva, 1947, pp. 201-2. (1st ed., 1666-88.)

[20] Cennino Cennini, *The Book of the Art of Cennino Cennini*, tr. C. J. Herringham, London, 1899, p. 78.

[21] De Planet, *op.cit.*, p. 73 (passage dated May 31, 1843).

[22] *Ibid.*

IMITATION

So far, then, Delacroix would appear an outright foe of nature as a supplier of raw material for the artist. Typically, however, his attitude defies simple categories. He was endowed with the ability to appreciate both sides of every coin with a high degree of lucidity and, at times, one finds him advocating a healthy respect for nature and for artistic representation that did not stray too far from its natural inspiration.

As a very young man — at the age of twenty — he expressed in a letter to his friend Piron[23] a fundamental attachment to nature which he never abandoned. In this passage, he described the role of art as a mirror of nature (thus recalling the well-known image of Leonardo). In a burst of youthful enthusiasm he declared in October 1818: "Le bonheur de celui qui sent la nature, c'est de la rendre: heureux celui qui la réfléchit comme un miroir, qui fait la chose pour amour de la chose et non pas avec la prétention de la faire mieux qu'un autre."[24] This pleasure in the depiction of visual reality is apparent in a number of studies of nude figures which reflect his early conquest of Academic procedures gleaned from his studies with Guérin and at the Ecole des Beaux-Arts. *Seated Nude: Mademoiselle Rose* of 1821-23 (Fig. 11) renders with great suavity of contour and modeling the pliant flesh of the voluptuous and languorous Mademoiselle Rose, one of his favorite models at this time. Apart from the faint expression of anxiety evident in the eyes, this rendering of the female nude form offers a faithful and objective account with absolutely no attempt to beautify, idealize, or recast according to a preordained canon of proportions. It is, in every way, an image that anticipates the realism that will triumph with Courbet about thirty years later. Delacroix, however, was destined to abandon such unadorned statements; yet, even in his

23 E. A. Piron, the executor of Delacroix's estate, was also the author of one of the first substantial books on the artist: *Eugène Delacroix: sa vie et ses œuvres*, Paris, 1865.

24 *Correspondance générale*, v, p. 2 (from a letter to Piron which is dated by Joubin, October 1818). Leonardo's criterion of judgment for painting as a mirror image of nature occurs frequently in the *Treatise on Painting*, as for example: "When you wish to see whether your painting altogether conforms with the thing drawn from nature, take a mirror and reflect the living thing in it. Compare the thing reflected with your picture and consider well whether the subject of both representations is in conformity in both cases." Leonardo da Vinci, *Treatise on Painting*, I, p. 160.

most imaginative efforts, this sound training in the exact rendering of the model will always be felt.

That he never abandoned his fundamental respect for nature is indicated in a letter of 1859 wherein he still advocated strict observance of nature as the secret basis of his art: "Vous me demandez si j'ai un secret: il est le même que celui des gens, malheureusement en petit nombre, dont la plus grande finesse consiste à dire toujours la vérité. On nous a trop répété qu'il est certains artifices sans lesquels la peinture ne peut avoir toute sa valeur. En observant bien la nature, qui ne fait pas d'efforts pour produire de l'effet, on s'aperçoit que c'est à la suivre pas à pas plutôt qu'à ajouter ou à corriger qu'il faut s'appliquer."[25] A preparatory sketch (Fig. 12) for one of the figures of the Salon of Peace of the Hôtel de Ville of Paris (begun in 1852, completed in 1854, and destroyed by fire in 1871) demonstrates that, in the 1850's, as a mature artist, he still rooted his art in a faithful study of nature. The sensitive, rippling contours and the subtle modeling of anatomical detail reveal a formidable command of naturalistic representation.

Elsewhere, in the same decade, he recorded further interest in this topic by welcoming with great enthusiasm the development of photography, which he felt would furnish artists new insights for the adequate representation of natural objects. "Combien je regrette," he declared, "qu'une si admirable invention arrive si tard, je dis pour ce qui me regarde! La possibilité d'étudier d'après de semblables résultats eût eu sur moi une influence dont je me fais une idée seulement par l'utilité dont ils me sont encore . . . c'est la démonstration palpable du vrai dessin de la nature, dont nous n'avons jamais autrement que des idées bien imparfaites."[26] It is a matter of record that he actually put into practice the use of this new medium: there exist drawings by his hand made after photographs which reveal his attempt to capitalize upon the new device.[27]

[25] From a letter of April 18, 1859, to M. Pérignon; see *Correspondance générale*, IV, p. 94.

[26] From a letter of March 7, 1854, to Constant Dutilleux; see *Correspondance générale*, III, p. 196.

[27] For an example of these drawings, see R. Escholier, *Delacroix: peintre, graveur, écrivain*, Paris, 1926, III, illustration opposite p. 200; see also B. Newhall, "Delacroix and Photography," *Magazine of Art*, 45 (Nov. 1952), pp. 300-3.

The nature of his use of these photographs has been described by his friend, the painter Constant Dutilleux, who indicated that he "n'admirait pas les photographies seulement en théoricien . . . il dessina considérablement d'après des plaques daguerriennes et des épreuves sur papier."[28] Moreover, he tells us that Delacroix did not regard these photographs merely as objects to be copied: "Le rayonnement de l'idéal qu'il portait en lui transformait en héros vaincus et rêveurs, nymphs nerveuses et pantelantes des modèles à trois francs la séance." In his view, photographic material provided welcome substitutes for models. But like the reality which they imaged, they were regarded as nothing but the indispensable point of departure — the point of departure from which artistic inspiration embarked. He had nothing but scorn for those unimaginative souls who were content with the unadorned recording of the facts of nature. In the Journal, on October 12, 1853, he spoke of the imitation of nature as "ce grand point de départ de toutes les écoles et sur lequel elles se divisent profondément, aussitôt qu'elles l'interprètent, toute la question semble réduite à ceci: l'imitation est-elle faite en vue de plaire à l'imagination ou de satisfaire simplement une sorte de conscience d'une singulière espèce, qui consiste, pour l'artiste, à être content de lui quand il a copié, aussi exactement que possible, le modèle qu'il a sous les yeux?"[29]

It is in his conception of what justifies departure from nature that Delacroix emerges as a man of his age, that is to say, a Romantic. Whereas theoreticians of the Renaissance and the seventeenth century had sanctioned a departure from nature in the direction of embellishment or improvement, embodied (in France) in the concept of "la belle nature,"[30] Romantic aesthetics advocated a new treatment of nature, which now became subservient to the dictates of the imagination and the subjective interpretation of the individual artist. But, as we shall see, the triumph of this point of view, to which Delacroix contributed, was prepared by eighteenth-century writers whose works he knew.

[28] From unpublished notes of Dutilleux; quoted by Escholier, *op.cit.*, III, p. 202.
[29] *Journal*, II, p. 88.
[30] See above p. 49, n. 13.

Quite appropriately, Delacroix cites as authority for his ultimate departure from the initial inspiration of nature a work of that fountainhead of Romanticism, Jean-Jacques Rousseau. Apropos of landscape (and it is well to recall that by this time the conception of plein-air painting had already been advocated in France[31]), Delacroix, in 1853, welcomed the words of Rousseau in this manner: "Jean-Jacques dit avec raison qu'on peint mieux les charmes de la liberté quand on est sous les verrous, qu'on décrit mieux une campagne agréable quand on habite une ville pesante et qu'on ne voit le ciel que par une lucarne et à travers les cheminées."[32] This is a paraphrase of a passage of *Les confessions* which stated: "Si je veux peindre le printemps, il faut que je sois en hiver; si je veux décrire un beau paysage, il faut que je sois dans des murs. . . ."[33]

In this matter, one might note that Addison, in the *Spectator* paper of June 21, 1712, while extolling the pleasures of the imagination, had expressed a similar sentiment along with an analogous image of confinement: "We cannot indeed have a single Image in the Fancy that did not make its Entrance through the Sight: but we have the power of retaining, altering and compounding those Images, which we have once received, into all the Varieties of Picture and Vision that are most agreeable to the Imagination; for by this Faculty a Man in a Dungeon is capable of entertaining himself with Scenes and Landskips more beautiful than any that can be found in the whole Compass of Nature."[34]

The beneficial work of the imagination, aided by time, in the transformation of the initial inspiration into something that might appeal more strongly to the spectator's imagination was also described by Delacroix. In practice, he not only opposed plein-air painting of landscapes but also a strict adherence in the studio to sketches made after nature. It was, in his view, such exactitude

[31] See the discussion of plein-air painting in France before 1830 by Robert L. Herbert, *Barbizon Revisited*, New York, 1962, pp. 19-20.

[32] *Journal*, II, p. 91 (October 17, 1853).

[33] Quoted by Frederick C. Green, *Jean-Jacques Rousseau: A Critical Study of his Life and Writings*, Cambridge, 1955, p. 43.

[34] Addison, Joseph and Richard Steele, *The Spectator*, ed. G. Gregory Smith, New York, 1909, III, vol. 6, p. 56. It is worth noting that Rousseau, in *Les Confessions*, acknowledged approval of the *Spectator* papers: "Le *Spectateur* surtout me plut beaucoup et me fit du bien." Jean-Jacques Rousseau, *Les Confessions*, Paris, 1912, p. 159.

that had spoiled Courbet's background for the *Bathers* of 1853 (Fig. 3).[35] "Quand Courbet a fait le fond de la femme qui se baigne," he wrote, "il l'a copié scrupuleusement d'après une étude que j'ai vue à côté de son chevalet. Rien n'est plus froid; c'est un ouvrage de marqueterie."[36] Citing his own experience, he then explains why the result resembled inlaid woodwork: "Je n'ai commencé à faire quelque chose de passable, dans mon voyage d'Afrique, qu'au moment où j'avais assez oublié les petits détails pour ne me rappeler dans mes tableaux que le côté frappant et poétique; jusque-là, j'étais poursuivis par l'amour de l'exactitude, que le plus grand nombre prend pour la vérité." In order to capture the striking and poetic side of things — or, in other words, that subjective, intangible essence which constitutes for the Romantic artist true reality — Delacroix advocated the operation of time, the effacer of the petty details which obscure the desired effect. This conception, no doubt, accounts, in part, for his frequent repetition of favorite themes throughout his life.[37]

A vivid illustration of this procedure exists in the two pictures he executed on the subject of Algerian women in their apartment. With his theory in mind it is possible to explain and, perhaps, to appreciate more fully the 1849 variant in the Museum of Montpellier in relation to the more famous version in the Louvre which is dated 1834.

Observe, to begin with, that even the first version was executed two years after the event which inspired it — the famous voyage to North Africa of 1832. There he energetically filled his notebooks with material, written and pictorial, that would serve, once returned to France, as another dictionary or source of objects and themes rooted in the visual perception of nature recorded on the site.[38] Later, in France, the effect of time and memory was to work

[35] See above p. 18 and n. 23.

[36] *Journal*, II, pp. 91-92 (October 17, 1853).

[37] Consider, for example, the *Medea* which exists in versions of 1838 (Lille Museum), 1856 (Berlin Museum), and two in 1862 (Louvre and Collection Vicomtesse de Noailles, Paris).

[38] For Delacroix's trip to Morocco, see especially: *Le voyage de Eugène Delacroix au Maroc*, introduction by J. Guiffrey, Paris, 1909; J. Alazard, "Les peintres de l'Algérie au XIXe siècle," *Gazette des Beaux-Arts*, VIe (June 1930), pp. 370-87; and *L'Orient et la peinture française au XIXe siècle, d'E. Delacroix à Auguste Renoir*, Paris, 1930; André Joubin, ed., *Eugène Delacroix: voyage*

the transformation of these literal notes into finished products which exuded poetic and Romantic atmosphere.

Fortunately, we possess water-color studies of Algerian women (Fig. 14) made on the spot which amply demonstrate his ability to record in a rapid and literal way what he actually observed. Further insight into the original nature of the physical environment of the women can be gleaned from another sketch (Fig. 13) made in Algiers. Here, devoid of human presence, one discovers the inspiration for many of the artifacts—Moorish arch, tiles, cabinet, and mirror — that found their way into the final picture. Again, as though he did not trust the medium of water color to render the particular quality of the color experience, Delacroix supplies, as in the previous sketches, written references to the colors of the objects. Thus, while possessing a certain winsome and lively quality that make them quite delightful in their own right, these studies exist primarily on the level of literal fact.

After an appreciable removal in place and time, the finished painting based on these sketches (Fig. 15) reveals a remarkable mixture of fidelity to fact as first recorded in the sketches and the imposition of a romantic and mysterious content. Factual, since faithful to the sketches, are the very poses of the women, the basic nature of their dress, the oblique interior space and many aspects of the furnishing and decoration of the room. Surprisingly, in view of his distaste of petty detail, the finished picture supplies more detailed information than the sketches: What had been merely suggested about the clothing and decoration has now acquired precise description, especially with the addition of floor tiles, a definite pattern in the wall tiles, and the rugs on which the women sit. The very medium of oil paint invites this proliferation of detail; for Delacroix, however, these elements very probably had value chiefly as exotic items that heightened the romantic aura of the presentation. As in so many of his pictures the realistic basis only served to render more cogently the intangible and essential content.

With his conception of the function of memory and time in mind, it is instructive to analyze the transformation that occurs

au Maroc, Paris, 1930; and René Hardy, "La double révélation du voyage en Afrique," in René Huyghe et al., Delacroix, Paris, 1963, pp. 137-56.

when he takes up the theme fifteen years later, in 1849. Certain writers have professed to see in the Montpellier picture (Fig. 16) a closer adherence to the original inspiration attributable to his desire to refresh his memory concerning certain details.[39] However, there can be little doubt that Delacroix, in accordance with his stated idea, actually suppressed a number of important details which had contributed to the sense of exotic reality in the Louvre picture. The tiles of the floor and the wall have disappeared; the dress of the women (especially those in the middle distance) has lost that broad, yet descriptive depiction of Moorish pattern; the still-life elements have decreased in number; and everything has been rendered in a more generalized technique that tends to obliterate detail and local color, this despite the fact that certain parts of the picture retain a high degree of brilliant illumination. As a result, the picture loses a great deal of the exotic, localized charm of the earlier version. Yet, by the suppression of detail under the erosive effect of time, it achieves, by way of compensation, a more striking and poetic power in which the languor and lassitude inherent in the theme gain an aura of pathos which adds further poetic dimension to this evocation of harem life.

The "striking and poetic effect" which Delacroix sought to achieve in his works had its origin, of course, within the artist himself; that is, in good Romantic fashion, he injects subjective content into a scene based on visual reality. Recall that he had once voiced an appeal to the artist to approach the subjective and unique ideal within him rather than to record the transitory ideal which nature presents.[40] This willingness to clothe reality in a subjective guise constitutes a cornerstone of his art, but one that had already evolved in the works of two of his most stimulating sources — Diderot and Madame de Staël. The former, in his *Pensées*

[39] Elie Lambert, "L'Appartement des femmes d'Alger et les albums de voyage d'Eugène Delacroix au Maroc," *La Revue de l'art*, LXV (May 1934), pp. 187-91. Lambert cites a similar opinion expressed by Georges Marçais in his *Le costume musulman d'Alger*, Paris, 1930. Marçais' proof seems to lie principally in what he claims to be the more naturalistic motivation for the light source. Both Lambert and Marçais seem to strain for positivistic explanations to the point where they appear blind to the greater departure from the initial sketches in the Montpellier picture. On this subject, see also Elie Lambert, *Delacroix et les Femmes d'Alger*, Paris, 1937.

[40] See above pp. 47-48 and n. 5.

détachées sur la peinture, had formulated a subjective interpretation of imitation as part of his campaign to introduce new subject matter and content into what he considered the decadent and empty art of the courtly tradition: "Cette imitation, où en est le modèle? dans l'âme, dans l'esprit, dans l'imagination plus ou moins vive, dans le cœur plus ou moins chaud de l'auteur."[41] And, within that long passage which he quoted from Madame de Staël's *De l'Allemagne*,[42] the depiction of the inner sentiments of the soul took priority over fidelity to nature: "L'homme a dans son âme des sentiments innés, que les objets réels ne satisferont jamais, et c'est à ces sentiments que l'imagination des peintres et des poëtes sait donner une forme et une vie. Le premier des arts, la musique, qu'imite-il?"[43]

In theory, then, Delacroix demonstrably favored the expression of Romantic and subjective content by means of a transformation of nature into a new reality in the work of art, this transformation to be achieved by the suppression of details and a general disregard for exactitude with the aid of the passage of time. Addison, Jean-Jacques Rousseau, Diderot, and Madame de Staël furnished him theoretical foundations for the validity of subjective content and Rubens a practical working method that enabled the artist to transform, according to the dictates of his genius, the initial inspiration from nature. At the same time, like his Romantic predecessors, Gros and Géricault, he retained a strong respect for nature and frequently expressed, in theory as well as in practice, an almost Leonardesque reliance upon the fundamental importance of truth to nature in order to prevent a radical departure into the realm of imaginative fantasy.

The conscious articulation of this point of view takes on special significance in relation to the hostile criticism that greeted his technical innovations in the way of a general loosening of the tight, discreet brushwork advocated by the Academicians. One Jean Rousseau, for example, commenting on the Salon of 1859, discerned in Delacroix's contribution a disturbingly cavalier treat-

[41] Diderot, *Pensées détachées* (in *Essais sur la peinture*, pp. 202-3).

[42] See above p. 31 and n. 74.

[43] Hubert Gillot (*E. Delacroix: l'homme, ses idées, son œuvre*, p. 328) cites this passage as Delacroix's own in his discussion of the artist's attitude toward nature.

ment of subject matter: "Le temps est proche, — si Delacroix ne guérit, — où il ne s'exercera plus qu'à accoupler des tons sans s'inquiéter de représenter quelque chose, et à faire des bouquets où l'on ne trouvera pas même des fleurs."[44] To contemporary vision, the literary subject of one of the most progressive entries of Delacroix at the Salon of 1859, the *Abduction of Rebecca* (Fig. 17), may appear almost too obtrusive. However, it is not difficult to fathom why, for Rousseau in 1859, the late style of Delacroix as embodied in this work must have appeared alarmingly revolutionary indeed. Form, as conceived by the schools of David and Ingres, is now threatened by a deliberate denial of linear definition of contour, by the blurring of descriptive detail, by abandonment of traditional spatial construction, by the creation of a fluctuating and vibrant network of highlights across the surface of the canvas, and by the symphonic and fused color that abolishes the dictates of local color. There results a rendering of visual excitement which serves not only to create a dramatic visual equivalent for the theme of abduction but which also tends towards an abstract experience of color and movement. No wonder such a picture elicited from Rousseau a prophetic statement concerning Delacroix's role in the movement towards the destruction of the traditional treatment of subject matter — and, ultimately, subject matter itself — that would begin in the 1860's with Manet and continue with the Impressionists. This development was already anticipated by Delacroix when he recorded in the Journal in 1857 a willingness to abolish subject matter as conceived in the first half of the nineteenth century. "La peinture," he wrote, "n'a pas toujours besoin d'un sujet."[45] To be sure, on this occasion, he cited the example of Géricault, who had painted the very unacademic subject of dismembered arms and legs. Therefore, he was not advocating the utter dismissal of subject matter — a phenomenon that would occur only in the twentieth century. However, in view of his quotation of Madame de Staël's description of the intangible content of music and his own conception of the superiority of painting as due

[44] From a review of the Salon of 1859 published in the *Figaro* of Tuesday, May 10, 1859; quoted by Maurice Tourneux, *Eugène Delacroix devant ses contemporains*, Paris, 1886, p. 102.

[45] *Journal*, III, p. 24 (January 13, 1857).

to its ability to suggest content impossible in the medium of literature, it is not altogether inappropriate to discover in his theory and practice the seeds of contemporary interest in the rendering of intangible content without the benefit of recognizable subject matter.

THE IMITATION OF THE ANTIQUE

The characteristically ambivalent nature of Delacroix's thought, his ability to see in almost every case the two sides of any coin, is equally operative in his attitude towards imitation of the Antique. In view of his general hostility to the aesthetics of David and Ingres, one might have expected from him a corresponding hostility to one of their major tenets — the unassailable authority of Antique art. Quite the contrary; his admiration for the achievement of Antiquity turns out to be no less unstinting. Where he differs from their point of view appears in his interpretation of the true essence of Classicism — an interpretation that assumes importance for the nature of the classicizing elements of his own art.

His ardent admiration of Antique art can be found in numerous discussions in which, in a manner reminiscent of the traditional argument of Ancients versus Moderns,[46] he contrasts the advantages of modern and Antique art. On one occasion, he readily admitted that the Ancients had attained a pinnacle of perfection beyond the realm of contemporary achievement: " . . . c'est surtout dans tout ce qui nous reste des arts plastiques des anciens que cette qualité de goût et de mesure parfaite se trouve au plus haut point de perfection. Nous pouvons soutenir la comparaison avec eux dans la littérature; dans les arts, jamais."[47] Furthermore, Antique art, while maintaining a high level of perfection, never diluted its effects with the idiosyncratic qualities that often characterized post-Classical products: "L'antique ne sacrifie pas à la grâce, comme Raphaël, Corrège et la Renaissance en général; il n'a pas cette affectation, soit de la force, soit de l'imprévu, comme dans Michel-Ange."[48] Rather, it remained imperturbable in its serene and formally impeccable achievement: "L'antique est toujours égal,

---

[46] For bibliography on this topic, see above p. 17, n. 21.
[47] *Journal*, III, p. 57 (January 25, 1857).
[48] *Ibid.*, p. 58.

serein, complet dans ses détails et l'ensemble irréprochable en quelque sorte."[49] In all these tributes, he expressed nothing by way of attitude and interpretation that would have contradicted the Academic point of view.

His admiration was not, however, without certain reservations. Perfection, he held, posed its own disadvantages and modern art, in failing to achieve this condition, was free to attain certain qualities by way of compensation: "Il en est résulté nécessairement dans les âges modernes plus d'imperfection dans les qualités plastiques. Les anciens n'offrent point les exagérations ou incorrections des Michel-Ange, des Puget, des Corrège; en revanche, le beau calme de ces belles figures n'éveille en rien cette partie de l'imagination que les modernes intéressent par tant de points."[50] By relinquishing Classical ideals of order, measure, and perfection, in favor of exaggerations and lapses from correctness, modern art (i.e., post-Antique art) achieved a new and equally valid mode of expression in which a vague, intangible, and fundamentally inexplicable content becomes the prime concern of the artist. In the work of Michelangelo, for example, he detects an intriguing "je ne sais quoi de mystérieux et d'agrandi qui passionne son moindre ouvrage" and in Rembrandt "le vague, la magie, le dessin expressif."[51]

This ability to appreciate the contrasting virtues of both Ancient and modern art demonstrates once again the characteristic duality of his theoretical procedure. Fortunately, his clarity of perception was such that he never succumbed to chaos and confusion in a haphazard oscillation between these two poles; rather, in a highly rational and conscious manner, he endeavored to reconcile the Ancient and modern qualities, enjoying the benefits of both. Painting, he concluded, was more capable of such an accommodation than sculpture since it has superior means at its disposal: "La peinture dispose de tous les prestiges de la couleur et de ceux de la perspective, ignorée des anciens; elle réunit la précision et le vague, tout ce qui charme et tout ce qui frappe. On peut dire de

49 *Journal*, III, p. 173 (February 23, 1858).
50 *Journal*, III, p. 60 (January 25, 1857).
51 *Ibid.*

la peinture comme de la musique, qu'elle est essentiellement un art moderne."[52]

Delacroix, then, felt unreservedly committed to the expression of modern content — that intangible content which had already been suggested in antecedent theory by the term "je ne sais quoi," which, already in the seventeenth century, was characterized as something "more easily felt than known, its nature being incomprehensible and inexplicable; the heart instinctively perceives it; without it all attractive qualities are lifeless. . . . It is all a matter of feeling, not of reason."[53] Yet, he wanted nothing equivocal to hamper the spectator's realization of this content. Therefore he turned to the Classical mode of expression for aid in achieving precision in the physical rendering of this message. As a result, his attempt, in theory and in practice, to fuse the rational and the irrational by the ordered, clear, and precise depiction of the vague and mysterious realm of the "soul" informed a tempered kind of Romantic art that finds a certain parallel in the poetry of his ardent champion, Baudelaire, who already in the mid-nineteenth century described Delacroix as "passionnément amoureux de la passion, et froidement déterminé à chercher les moyens d'exprimer la passion de la manière la plus visible."[54]

While Delacroix's conception of the rational aspect of Antique art conformed well with the official dogma of the Academy, his characterization of modern art as involved with vague, subjective, and emotive forces owed much to the influence of German writers, especially the Schlegels, whose ideas on the subject were available to him in the masterwork of Madame de Staël.[55] Like her German predecessors she had attributed the origin of the modern, anticlassical point of view to the introduction of Christianity: "Les

[52] From his article "Des variations du beau," which appeared in the *Revue des Deux-Mondes*, July 15, 1857; see *Œuvres littéraires*, I, pp. 47-48.

[53] Samuel H. Monk's paraphrase of the conception of Dominique Bouhours as it appeared in *Les entretiens d'Ariste et d'Eugène* of 1671; see Monk, "A Grace Beyond the Reach of Art," p. 146.

[54] Baudelaire, "L'Œuvre et la vie d'Eugène Delacroix," p. 426.

[55] See Arthur O. Lovejoy, "On the Discrimination of Romanticisms," *PMLA*, XXXIX (January 1924), pp. 229-53. Lovejoy points out that it had early occurred to Friedrich Schlegel that "the principal historic cause of the supposed radical differentiation of modern from classical art could lie only in the influence of Christianity."

anciens avaient, pour ainsi dire, une âme corporelle, dont tous les mouvements étaient forts, directs et conséquents: il n'en est pas de même du cœur humain développé par le christianisme: les modernes ont puisé dans le repentir chrétien l'habitude de se replier continuellement sur eux-mêmes."[56] This conception of the external and objective orientation of Ancient art which accounted for its attainment of perfection, and of the introduction of Christianity which, according to Madame de Staël, had stimulated in the arts a need to manifest "cette existence tout intérieure" by means of a more subtle expression, a less perfect visualization in order to capture "les émotions intimes et multipliées dont notre âme est susceptible" — found its way into Delacroix's theory. In a long passage on the Antique which he entered in the Journal as a preparatory note for the projected *Dictionnaire des beaux-arts,* one discovers similar thoughts in what amounts to a paraphrase of Madame de Staël's statement. The Ancients are described as a people "chez lesquels la forme plastique extérieure passe avant l'expression. On explique par l'introduction du christianisme cette singulière révolution qui se fait au moyen âge dans les arts du dessin, c'est-à-dire la prédominance de l'expression. Le mysticisme chrétien qui planait sur tout, l'habitude pour les artistes de représenter presque exclusivement des sujets de la religion qui parlent, avant tout à l'âme, ont favorisé indubitablement cette pente générale à l'expression. Il en est résulté nécessairement dans les âges modernes plus d'imperfection dans les qualités plastiques."[57]

Although Delacroix fully appreciated the formal perfections of Ancient art, he differed radically from the interpretation of Classicism posed by the school of David. In view of his general hostility towards David this comes as no surprise. More unexpected, perhaps, is the solid foundation in traditional theory that bulwarked his attack upon the entrenched foe.

Delacroix, as we shall discover, never opposed the imitation of the Antique per se. What disturbed his aesthetic sensibility was "cette imitation souvent peu intelligente et exclusive" that he perceived among those Davidians who utterly failed to penetrate

---

56 De Staël, *De l'Allemagne,* p. 167.
57 *Journal,* III, pp. 59-60 (January 25, 1857).

the spirit of the Antique.[58] Paradoxically, one of the models of that school, Poussin, provided, in Delacroix's view, the exemplary approach to the problem: "Poussin n'a pas imité les bas-reliefs et les statues par le côté matériel, comme on l'a vu faire de nos jours, c'est-à-dire qu'il ne mettait pas un soin scrupuleux au costume, aux usages purement extérieurs."[59] That is to say, Poussin's Classicism revived the spirit that lay behind the conventions of Classical art and never degenerated into the antiquarianism which allegedly plagued lesser followers of the Classical persuasion. In this respect, he mirrored very closely the advice propounded by Roger de Piles who urged painters to regard "l'Antique comme un Livre qu'on traduit dans une autre Langue dans laquelle il suffit de bien rapporter le sens et l'esprit, sans s'attacher servilement aux paroles."[60]

De Piles, who abhorred the antiquarian Classicism of his own era, looked to Rubens (whose paintings he championed and whose treatise, *De imitatione antiquarum statuarum*, he translated and included in the *Cours de peinture par principes*,[61] which Delacroix knew) as the proper guide to the treatment of the Antique. Like de Piles, Delacroix was an ardent admirer of the Flemish master; his predilection for his energetic, turbulent, Baroque forms is well-known. Of equal interest is the fact that he revives in his theory the fundamental ideas concerning the proper imitation of Antique statues expounded by Rubens. Furthermore, he regarded Flemish art (along with that of Titian) as the modern exemplar of the true essence of Ancient art, asserting that "Titien et les Flamands ont l'esprit de l'antique et non l'imitation de ses formes extérieures."[62] For, like them, he was able to appreciate the more dynamic aspect of Ancient art. "Ce qui caractérise l'antique," he claimed, "c'est l'ampleur savante des formes combinée avec le sentiment de la

[58] In the same passage on David and his school, Delacroix remarked: "Au lieu de pénétrer l'esprit de l'antique et de joindre cette étude à celle de la nature, etc., on voit qu'il a été l'écho d'une époque où on avait la fantaisie de l'antique." *Journal*, III, p. 23 (January 13, 1857).

[59] From his article on Poussin which appeared in the *Moniteur universel*, June 26, 29, and 30, 1853; see *Œuvres littéraires*, II, p. 95.

[60] Roger de Piles, *Abrégé de la vie des peintres*, Paris, 1699, p. 25.

[61] See Roger de Piles, *Cours de peinture par principes*, pp. 139-47.

[62] *Journal*, III, p. 58 (January 25, 1857).

vie. . . ."[63] Moreover, this breadth and liveliness effectively contradicted, in his view, the dry, cold interpretations of the Antique that had been fostered by the Winckelmann-Mengs-David-Ingres tradition. "La véritable esprit de l'antique," he insisted, "ne consiste pas à donner à toute figure isolée l'apparence d'une statue."[64]

Rubens, in the *De imitatione antiquarum statuarum*, had cautioned against the exact imitation of Antique marbles in painting to the point of exclusion of inspiration from nature; it could rightly be claimed of artists of this persuasion that "au lieu d'imiter la chair, ils ne représentent que du marbre teint de diverses couleurs."[65] This cautionary advice was repeated by other voices, especially during the eighteenth century. Roger de Piles revived its argument in his effort to inject new life into Academic formulae, asserting that "le naturel a toujours quelque chose de vif et de remuant qui tempère cette immobilité des figures antiques; et ceux qui prennent trop de soin de les imiter, sans prendre garde aux graces particulières qui accompagnent la nature vivante, tombe toujours dans la sécheresse."[66] Even Diderot, who generally deplored the sensuality of the courtly tradition, repeated for his avid reader Delacroix the familiar words of warning: "Celui qui aura négligé la nature pour l'antique, risquera d'être froid, sans vie, sans aucunes de ces vérités cachées et secrètes, qu'on n'aperçoit que dans la nature même."[67] This attitude naturally gathered its most enthusiastic adherents among those opponents of the alleged lifelessness, dryness, and coldness of the school of David. One of these writers was quoted in 1860 by the aging Delacroix, who derived a long passage from Vitet's article on Pindar in the *Revue des Deux-Mondes* concerning this phenomenon. The Caylus-Winckelmann influence, according to Vitet, had encouraged in David and his followers the cultivation of "la sécheresse, la maigreur, et l'aridité," and was all the more unfortunate since the true nature of Greek

---

[63] From his article on Prud'hon which appeared in the *Revue des Deux-Mondes*, November 1, 1846; see *Œuvres littéraires*, II, p. 143.

[64] *Ibid.*

[65] De Piles, *Cours de peinture par principes*, p. 141.

[66] Roger de Piles, "Conversations sur la peinture," *Recueil de divers ouvrages sur la peinture et le coloris*, Paris, 1755, p. 38.

[67] From his Salon of 1765; see *Œuvres complètes de Diderot*, x, p. 418.

art lay in its liveliness: "C'était tout simplement la vie, la vie dans sa juste mesure, en parfait équilibre, avec l'ordre et la règle, mais avant tout, la vie. . . ."[68]

Delacroix's conception of the Antique as vital and dynamic accounts, no doubt, for his remarkable reaction to the natives of North Africa, in whom he discovered not only the essence of exoticism and mystery but also the very image of Antiquity. "Imagine, mon ami," he wrote in a letter to his friend, Pierret, from Tangier (February 29, 1832), "ce que c'est que de voir couchés au soleil, se promenant dans les rues, raccommodant des savates, des personnages consulaires, des Catons, des Brutus, auxquels il ne manque même pas l'air dédaigneux que devaient avoir les maîtres du monde . . . L'antique n'a rien de plus beau."[69]

Many of Delacroix's sketches executed in North Africa illustrate this insight. In particular, a watercolor, *Arab Women at a Fountain*, now in the Louvre (Fig. 18), emphasizes the luminosity of the Moorish dress, which he had compared in the same letter with ancient togas, "tout cela en blanc comme les sénateurs de Rome et les Panathénées d'Athènes." The figure on the right assumes a Poussinesque dignity and repose, almost statuesque in quality. Moreover, the background wall establishes a plane parallel to the picture plane — one of the clichés of the Neo-Classical style, characteristic of the relief-like compositions of David as well as of Poussin. And a perceptible idealization of the female type lends a certain nobility to the heads. On the other hand, the sketch possesses vivifying elements which imbue it with movement and spontaneity. The draperies, rejecting classical order and repose, either flow in liquid contours or describe rapid, angular movements that generate energy and force. At the same time, a vibrant wash models and animates the flesh tones evoking the impression of extraordinary health and vigor. This is Antiquity seen in terms of contemporary Africa and endowed with a Rubensian dynamism.

Contrary to the thesis of those who profess to see in Delacroix's work a break between the ardent romanticism of youth and the

[68] L. Vitet, "Pindare et l'art grec," *Revue des Deux-Mondes*, xxv (Feb. 1860), p. 720. Delacroix's quotation occurs in the *Journal*, iii, p. 261 (February 3, 1860).

[69] *Correspondance générale*, i, p. 319.

temperate classicism of maturity[70] is the evidence of his youthful interest in representations of Antique subject matter in Classical form.[71] The most interesting of these, in the light of his art theory, are, perhaps, his many sketches of Classical coins. One drawing of 1825, now in the Louvre (Fig. 19), which represents six ancient coins, well demonstrates his dictum: "Ce qui caractérise l'antique, c'est l'ampleur savantes des formes combinée avec le sentiment de la vie. . . ."[72] Obviously these coins interested him not for their archeological detail but, rather, the opportunity they afforded for the depiction of plastic and living forms which he endows with a potentiality of action that the originals possess only to a moderate degree. They demonstrate in practice the long tradition in theory, stemming from Rubens and de Piles, which opposed the overly faithful rendering of sculptural effects in painting.[73]

The happy result of Delacroix's exercises in the copying of ancient coins as well as his adherence to the Rubensian conception of the proper use of the Antique shows most successfully, perhaps, in the decoration of the Salon of the King of the Palais Bour-

[70] Recall the opinion of Raymond Escholier cited in the Introduction, p. 6.

[71] See the drawings of Classical subjects in Neo-Classical style, *Anacreon and Cupid, The Death of Drusus*, etc., all from Delacroix's student days dating before 1820, reproduced by Maurice Sérullaz, *Eugène Delacroix: dessins, aquarelles et lavis*, Paris, 1952, pls. II and III. Also notable are the Classical representations of the seasons designed as decoration of Talma's house in Paris in 1821 according to Lee Johnson, "Delacroix's Decorations for Talma's Dining Room," *Burlington Magazine*, XCIX (March 1957), pp. 78-89. For further use of Classical models by Delacroix, see Walter Pach, "Notes sur le classicisme de Delacroix," *L'Amour de l'art*, 1930, pp. 241-53; B. H. Polak, "De invloed van enige monumenten der Oudheid op het classicisme van David, Ingres en Delacroix," *Nederlandsch kunsthistorisch Jaarboek*, 1948-49, pp. 287-315; Charles Picard, "Les emprunts antiques de David, Ingres et Delacroix," *Revue d'archéologie*, XL, 1952, pp. 105 ff.; and Pach, "Le classicisme de Delacroix," *La revue des arts*, II (June 1952), pp. 109-12, and *The Classical Tradition in Modern Art*, New York, 1959, pp. 20-36.

[72] *Œuvres littéraires*, II, p. 143. See Charles Seltman, *Greek Coins*, London, 1933, pls. XX (nos. 1-4) and XXXIII (no. 14) for the type of coins of Tarentum that must have served as models for Delacroix.

[73] It is worth noting that, copying ancient coins, Delacroix consciously or not, followed the advice of Du Fresnoy, who had recommended this procedure in his *De arte graphica*: "Ce qu'il y a ici à faire, c'est d'imiter, le beau Naturel, comme ont fait les Anciens, tel que l'objet et la Nature de la chose le demandent: Et c'est pour cela que vous serez soigneux de rechercher les Médailles antiques . . . parce qu'elles nous donnent de grandes idées, et nous font produire de belles choses." Charles Alphonse Du Fresnoy, *L'Art de peinture*, tr. Roger de Piles, Paris, 1751, p. 31. (1st ed., 1667.)

bon (commissioned in 1833 and completed in 1838). *The Rhône*
(Fig. 20), painted in grisaille, retains the solidity and relief of a
piece of sculpture; yet, by means of a subtle yet powerful modeling,
the figure seems imbued with enormous energy and vitality. Obviously, then, Classicism, evoked in the 1830's and already practiced in both content and style in the 1820's, was not a vagary of
Delacroix's old age; nor was it initially inspired by his trip to
Africa. In subject matter and in form, it appeared early and remained a constant preoccupation throughout his life.

So far, we have emphasized his interest in what might be termed,
after Nietzsche, the Dionysiac aspect of Ancient art. But, while, at
times, prone to conceive of the Antique as a vital, dynamic entity
(partly, no doubt, in reaction to what he considered the frigid
Classicism of David and his followers) he was able, characteristically, to appreciate the more formal aspects of Ancient art and,
furthermore, to utilize them in his own art. The traditional
Winckelmann conception of the Antique as calm, ordered, noble,
and serene[74] was not entirely alien to him. Consider, for example,
his statement of January 13, 1857: "J'appellerais volontiers classiques tous les ouvrages réguliers, ceux qui satisfont l'esprit non
seulement par une peinture exacte ou grandiose ou piquante des
sentiments et des choses, mais encore par l'unité, l'ordonnance
logique, en un mot par toutes ces qualités qui augmentent
l'impression en amenant la simplicité."[75] These qualities of unity,
order, and simplicity could provide valuable elements of that restraint he felt necessary to insure the maximum power of expression. He perceived acutely the dangerous pitfalls of Romantic
excess and feared lest his ardent but subjective language might
become incoherent without a clear and unambiguous formal presentation. Even in Rubens, whom he idolized in most respects, he
discerned failings on this score. After examining an etching of one
of Rubens' hunt pictures, he declared, "Tout cela est fait pour

[74] "The noble simplicity and silent grandeur of Greek statues are also truly
characteristic of Greek literature of the best period, that is, the writings of the
school of Socrates. These traits, more than anything else, give Raphael the
greatness that he attained through using the ancients for his models." Johann
J. Winckelmann, "Thoughts on the Imitation of Greek Art in Painting and
Sculpture" (1755), ed. and tr. Elizabeth Gilmore Holt, *Literary Sources of Art
History*, Princeton, 1947, p. 534.
[75] *Journal*, III, p. 23 (January 13, 1857).

frapper l'imagination, et l'exécution est admirable. Mais l'aspect est confus, l'œil ne sait où se fixer, il a le sentiment d'un affreux désordre, mais il semble que l'art n'y a pas assez présidé, pour augmenter par une prudente distribution ou par des sacrifices l'effet de tant d'inventions de génie."[76]

On at least one occasion he incorporated into his work a correction of Rubens' "disorder." In his late *Lion Hunt* of 1861 (Fig. 21) he treated a theme recurrent in his own œuvre, a theme which continues the tradition established by Rubens as in his *Lion Hunt* of 1616-17 (Fig. 22). In both, men encounter snarling, savage beasts in close physical combat. In both, the drama of fierce struggle is enhanced by pictorial devices: diagonal lines, fluttering curvilinear contours, assertive colors, and a free, active brushstroke. Both achieve a remarkable degree of intensity. Delacroix, however, generates dramatic power while departing from Rubens' inspiration in one significant way. Where Rubens relishes the complexity and confusion of the subject, Delacroix, though maintaining visual excitement, rejects the disarray. He ingeniously clarifies the action by introducing an elliptical pattern round which his groups form. He separates individual actions one from the other so that three major focal points of struggle emerge clearly where Rubens had concentrated his figures in one seething mass. In other words he expresses the turbulence and violence of the theme — but in the clearest, most orderly fashion possible.

His sensitivity in this matter revealed itself not only during the years of maturity but as early as 1824 when he noted in the Journal: "Ce qui me fait plaisir, c'est que j'acquiers de la raison, sans perdre l'émotion excitée par le beau. Je désire bien ne pas me faire illusion: mais il me semble que je travaille plus tranquillement qu'autrefois. . . ."[77] This growing power of his reason to restrain an inherent excitability failed, in the eyes of his critics at least, to find a corresponding power of formal unity in the works he submitted to the Salons in the 1820's. For, had he not been sufficiently aware of this problem, these critics would have brought it very sharply to his attention. Apropos of the *Death of Sardanapalus* (Fig. 6) one writer, in the *Moniteur Universel*, suggested that "il est

[76] *Journal*, I, p. 168 (January 25, 1847).
[77] *Journal*, I, p. 53 (February 27, 1824).

temps encore de s'arrêter dans une telle carrière; que M. Delacroix mette un frein salutaire à son imagination pittoresque; qu'il s'efforce d'acquérir du style, qu'il consent à dessiner; qu'il mette son langage à la hauteur de ses pensées. . . ."[78] And, another, the leader of the anti-Delacroix faction, Delécluze, declared that a hopeless formlessness, the result of a lack of intellectual control, accounted for the alleged failure of this painting: " . . . l'intelligence du spectateur n'a pu pénétrer dans un sujet dont tous les détails sont isolés, où l'œil ne peut débrouiller la confusion des lignes et des couleurs. . . ."[79] The fundamentally hostile attitude of these writers to the young artist and their inability to recognize the nature of his problem of expression utterly prevented them, of course, from anticipating the achievement in the 1830's of the monumental Salon of the King, where Classical subject matter and Classical principles of formal unity, the fruit of Delacroix's effort to discipline his imaginative and intuitive propensities, combine to demonstrate his mastery of the traditionally approved aspects of Classical art.

Delacroix, then, refused to adhere exclusively to one interpretation of the Antique. He perceived both the Apollonian aspect espoused by the Winckelmann tradition and the more Dionysiac element celebrated in art by Rubens and articulated in writing by both Rubens and Roger de Piles. In his attempt to instill new life into what he considered the sterile Classicism of David and his followers, he revived the lively and dynamic interpretation of the latter personalities. On the other hand, he eagerly assimilated the lessons in formal expression that Classical art had to offer. For he never intended his own art, however vague and inchoate its subjectively induced content, to founder on the shoals of incomprehensibility. His intense effort to render classically clear the romantically vague determined the peculiar nature of his art, which evokes the image of an artistic personality exploiting the deepest resources of both intellect and feeling.

[78] From an article signed "Ch." of February 27, 1828, in the *Moniteur universel*; quoted by Tourneux, *Eugène Delacroix devant ses contemporains*, p. 49.

[79] Delécluze, in the *Journal des débats* of December 20, 1827; quoted by Tourneux, *op.cit.*, p. 49.

CHAPTER III

THE CREATIVE PROCESS

PERHAPS THE MOST extraordinary aspect of Delacroix's art theory is that which treats the creative process. For, while eloquent and comprehensive discussions of the nature of painting and the role of imitation abound in the history of art theory, it remained for the Romantic period to explore more thoroughly the mysterious and subjective elements of the genesis of the work of art. In this field the extensive treatment Delacroix devotes to such crucial topics as imagination, finish, genius, rules, and boldness acquires special significance, not only as a document in the history of Romantic aesthetics but also as the product of an artist intimately involved in the drama of the creative act. Furthermore, his exquisite awareness of the complex and subtle facets of this phenomenon coupled with the unique clarity of his vision enabled him to shed valuable light on the creative origin and development of his own art. As a result, one can clearly discern that he did not theorize merely on the basis of his practice; rather, he mingled with the results of practical experience ideas enunciated by earlier art theorists. Moreover, he flatly contradicts those authorities on his art who pose a dichotomy between his rational theory and his irrational expression. As we shall discover, he valued the "Classical" and the "Romantic" aspects of artistic creation, both of which he considered necessary for the proper evolution of an effective work of art.

IMAGINATION

Consider, to begin, that faculty with which he has been universally credited — the power of imagination. When Baudelaire wrote that for Delacroix "l'imagination était le don le plus précieux, la faculté la plus importante,"[1] he merely echoed the sentiments of the artist himself, who had once decisively stated: *"Imagination. Elle est la première qualité de l'artiste."*[2] Such wholehearted commitment to the sovereignty of this Romantic deity would seem to suggest a belief in the irrational inspiration of creation. Typically, however, Delacroix's allegiance in this matter is not undivided. Although he valued highly the operation of the imagination, he never intended to abandon himself completely to its dictates without observing the compensatory restraint of rational control. Examples in the realms of both the visual arts and literature provided evidence of the dangers of the workings of the unbridled imagination. Rubens, whose works he generally admired, occasionally suffered under the domination of an imaginative faculty which engendered various faults: "Sa peinture, où l'imagination domine, est surabondante partout; ses accessoires sont trop faits; son tableau ressemble à une assemblée où tout le monde parle à la fois."[3] And he noted in the works of Edgar Allan Poe, whose morbidly imaginative effects he might have been expected to relish, an alien and reprehensible license that was in no way to be taken as a model for French artists, who by temperament and tradition were allied to a more Classical approach: "Il y a dans ces conceptions vraiments *extraordinaires,* c'est-à-dire *extra-humaines,* un attrait de fantastique qui est attribué à quelques natures du Nord ou de je ne sais où, mais qui est refusé, à coup sûr, à nos natures françaises. Ces gens-là ne se plaisent que dans ce qui est hors ou extra-nature: nous ne pouvons, nous autres, perdre à ce point l'équilibre, et la raison doit être de tous nos écarts."[4] The imagination, rather, was to be restrained from excessive flights of fancy by the power of reason, with intellect at all times exerting its tempering influence. As he firmly put it on one occasion: "Je fais cette observation et je corrobore toutes celles qui précèdent, c'est-à-dire la nécessité de beaucoup d'intelligence dans l'imagination. . . ."[5]

[1] Baudelaire, "L'Œuvre et la vie d'Eugène Delacroix," p. 427.
[2] *Journal,* III, p. 44 (January 25, 1857).
[3] *Journal,* II, p. 85 (October 12, 1853).
[4] *Journal,* II, p. 437 (April 6, 1856).
[5] *Journal,* II, pp. 86-87 (October 12, 1853). Compare William Wordsworth, in *The Prelude* (1805) where the imagination is described as "but another name for absolute power/ And clearest insight, amplitude of mind,/ And Reason in her most exalted mood." See *The Complete Poetical Works of William Words-*

This reassertion of the role of reason in the creative process challenged the position of purer Romantics such as Jean-Jacques Rousseau, who exalted freedom from the limited vistas of reason and wrote to the Marquis de Mirabeau on January 31, 1767: ". . . la fatigue même de penser me devient chaque jour plus pénible. J'aime à rêver, mais librement, en laissant errer ma tête et sans m'asservir à aucun sujet. . . ."[6] Even more suspect to Delacroix would have been the dictum of Chateaubriand who had asserted, in *Génie du Christianisme* (1802), that "la peinture, l'architecture, la poésie et la grand éloquence ont toujours dégénéré dans les siècles philosophiques. C'est que l'esprit raisonneur, en détruisant l'imagination, sape les fondements des beaux-arts."[7] And, by his adherence to reason, Delacroix tempered the advice of Madame de Staël, otherwise his acknowledged mentor, when she was wont to describe the imagination as "la prêtresse de la nature."[8]

French art and literary criticism offered Delacroix a consistent and durable tradition for the primacy of reason as an element in the creative process. Boileau, in *L'Art poétique*, which the painter knew intimately and often quoted,[9] argues that reason nourishes rather than stifles poetry: "Au joug de la raison sans peine elle fléchit,/Et, loin de la gêner, la sert et l'enrichit."[10] Of greater interest, in the light of Delacroix's distaste for the fantastic flights of Poe's fancy, is the nature of Dubos' warning against the dangers of the enflamed imagination in poets who are "pleins de verve, mais qui n'ont jamais peint la nature, parce qu'ils l'ont coppiée d'après les vains phantômes que leur imagination brûlée en avait formés. . . ."[11] A word of caution from Voltaire was actually copied by the artist, who derived from the *Questions sur l'Encyclopédie*

---

worth, Boston, 1910, III, p. 314. René Huyghe, *Delacroix*, p. 239, attributes to the influence of the concept of Dandyism the balance of reason and emotion sought by Delacroix: "This equilibrium . . . is his Dandyism. . . . To attain this fullness involves the cultivation both of the imagination, which responds to what is welling up in the depths of us, and the reason, which gives it embodiment."

6 *Œuvres complètes de J. J. Rousseau*, Paris, 1833, XVI, p. 274.

7 François Auguste René Chateaubriand, "Génie du Christianisme," *Œuvres de M. le vicomte de Chateaubriand*, Paris, 1833, II, p. 295.

8 De Staël, *De l'Allemagne*, p. 491.

9 See *Journal*, II, p. 358 (July 18, 1855) for a quotation from the fourth book which treats the function of rules in the creative process.

10 *Œuvres complètes de Boileau Despréaux*, p. 242.

11 Dubos, *Réflexions critiques sur la poésie et sur la peinture*, II, p. 14.

a passage which declared that "la chose la plus rare est de joindre la raison avec l'enthousiasme; la raison consiste à voir toujours les choses comme elles sont. Celui qui dans l'ivresse voit les objets doubles est alors privé de la raison."[12]

Note that both Dubos and Voltaire had sounded the call to reason in order to prevent a flight from reality on the part of the unbridled imagination. How similar sounds Delacroix when in the concluding sentence of his paragraph on Poe he declares: "Il ne faut pas croire que ces auteurs-là aient plus d'imagination que ceux qui se contentent de décrire les choses comme elles sont, et il est certainement plus facile d'inventer par ce moyen des situations frappantes, que par la route battue des esprits intelligents de tous les siècles."[13]

Another writer familiar to Delacroix, Roger de Piles, while fulfilling the role of liberator of French art from the more stifling strictures of the Academy and advocating the exploitation of the imagination, carefully prescribed a just balance between it and the power of reason. He urged those students who have mastered the essentials of their art to depart from the trodden paths and to exercise their personal geniuses in the treatment of novel subject matter "comme un vin nouveau qui exhale violemment ses fumées pour rendre avec le tems sa liqueur plus agréable, ils s'abandonnent à l'impétuosité de leur imagination."[14] Nevertheless, like Dubos and Voltaire, de Piles, while granting that there exist "des songes bizarres qui avec un peu de modération seroient capables de mettre beaucoup d'esprit dans la composition d'un Tableau,"[15] revealed the native French suspicion of an extravagant and irresponsible imagination: "Mais on peut dire aussi qu'il y a des productions qui sont des songes de fièvre chaude, lesquelles n'ont aucune liaison, et dont il faut éviter la dangéreuse extravagance."[16]

In this matter, it is well to recall that de Piles was one of the first to ascribe to Rubens strong imaginative powers. In the *Dissertation sur les ouvrages des plus fameux peintres*,[17] which Delacroix

---

[12] Voltaire, *Questions sur l'Encyclopédie*, II, Part v, p. 151. Delacroix's quotation appears in the *Supplément* of the *Journal*, III, p. 399.

[13] *Journal*, II, p. 438 (April 6, 1856).

[14] De Piles, *Cours de peinture par principes*, p. 63.

[15] *Ibid.*, pp. 117-18. [16] *Ibid.*, p. 118.

[17] Included in de Piles' *Recueil de divers ouvrages sur la peinture et le coloris*, pp. 236-86.

knew and quoted at length,[18] he discerns that quality in the Flemish master but, at the same time attributes to him a greater degree of rational control than Delacroix had. "Rubens," according to de Piles, "imaginoit vivement, prudemment et sçavamment, et l'on peut dire qu'en naissant la nature l'avoit abondamment pourvû de ce feu céleste que déroba Promethée, et qui est commun aux bons peintres et aux bons poëtes; et quoique son imagination fût féconde et que les objets s'y présentassent en foule, il ne s'en laissoit néanmoins pas accabler, son jugement et sa prudence en prenoient seulement ce qui devoit contribuer. . . ."[19]

Delacroix's approval of the traditional French limitation of the imagination by reason must not blind us, however, to the importance he attached to the more Romantic faculty. For though he deplored Poe's fantasies he was not, on the other hand, so committed to the rational limits of reality as to advocate the confinement of the imaginative inspiration. Especially on those occasions when he was exposed to the new Realist aesthetic he tended to adopt the opposite point of view. In the course of one of his lively diatribes against that movement he claimed, in a manner reminiscent of Madame de Staël, that "devant la nature elle-même, c'est notre imagination qui fait le tableau."[20] And, at another time, he did not hesitate to bring to the attention of the Realists the instructive example of great artists of the past, asserting that "il n'est pas bien difficile, en effet, de voir que les ouvrages de Raphaël, que ceux de Michel-Ange, du Corrège et de leurs plus illustres contemporains, doivent à l'imagination leur charme principal et que l'imitation du modèle y est secondaire et même tout à fait effacée."[21]

It seems clear, then, that Delacroix was seeking to achieve the right proportion of reason and imagination just as he was determined, in respect to the problems of imitation, to avoid the extremes of Courbet's Realism and Ingres' Mannerism.

[18] Delacroix, in his article on Prud'hon, had underscored those passages in which de Piles relates his efforts to overcome the prejudices of French opinion against the art of Rubens; see *Œuvres littéraires*, II, p. 153. This is one of the examples of his sympathetic response to beleaguered artists and critics of the past.

[19] De Piles, *op.cit.*, p. 257.

[20] *Journal*, III, p. 232 (September 1, 1859).

[21] *Journal*, III, p. 269 (February 22, 1860).

The general consistency of his point of view in relation to these problems of artistic creation is apparent in his definition of the imagination. For, just as he declined to indulge in the Romantic conception of the unlimited imagination he also retained in his definition of that faculty certain traditional elements that prohibited an absolutely pure conception of the creative imagination.

Perhaps the most succinct statement of the doctrine of the creative imagination can be found in Baudelaire, who claimed that the imagination "a créé, au commencement du monde, l'analogie et la métaphore. Elle décompose toute la création, et, avec les matériaux amassés et disposés suivant des règles dont on ne peut trouver l'origine que dans le plus profond de l'âme, elle crée un monde nouveau, elle produit la sensation du neuf."[22] Of course, this conception of the imagination as a creative power was not unprecedented in the history of art theory. André Félibien, for example, had already desired to discover in art "quelque nouvelle invention qui n'ait point encore esté veûë," and had professed the belief that "toute la force de ces belles inventions consiste dans la faculté imaginative. . . ."[23]

Now Delacroix not only attributed to the imagination certain creative powers but also identified the source of these powers in the characteristically Romantic area of the "soul" — that favorite breeding place of Romantic content according to those German aestheticians who had influenced him through the vehicle of Madame de Staël.[24] For his description of the imaginative process reads as follows: "Imaginer une composition, c'est combiner les éléments d'objets qu'on connaît, qu'on a vus, avec d'autres qui tiennent à l'intérieur même, à l'âme de l'artiste."[25] However, while the latter part of Delacroix's statement accords nicely with Romantic theory, the former prescription — "combiner les éléments d'objets qu'on connaît, qu'on a vus" — relies upon antecedent theory. As with the appeal to reason which various authorities cited as the antidote to radical departures from nature, there appeared in the seventeenth and eighteenth centuries definitions of the imagination which de-

22 From his Salon of 1859; see Baudelaire, *Curiosités esthétiques* . . . , p. 321.
23 André Félibien, *Entretiens sur les vies et sur les ouvrages des plus excellens peintres*, Paris, 1685-88, I, pp. 592-93.
24 See above p. 19, n. 30.   25 *Œuvres littéraires*, I, p. 58.

scribed the matter of imaginative thought as derived from exterior reality.

Roger de Piles, for one, had pointed out that "quelque brillante que soit nôtre imagination, elle ne peut produire que les choses dont nôtre esprit s'est rempli, et nôtre mémoire ne nous raporte que les idées de ce que nous savons et de ce que nous avons vû."[26] This insistence upon things seen as the raw material of imaginative content occurs again and again in eighteenth-century thought, especially in such important sources for Delacroix's theory as the works of Voltaire and Diderot. Voltaire, in his *Questions sur l'Encyclopédie*, denied the purely creative function of the imagination since "elle semble créer quand elle ne fait qu'arranger, car il n'est pas donné à l'homme de se faire des idées, il ne peut que les modifier."[27] And Diderot, who sounded the forthcoming triumph of the imagination in the Romantic period in his description of that faculty as "la qualité dominante du poëte," repeats the eighteenth-century formula: "L'imagination ne crée rien, elle imite, elle compose, combine, exagère, agrandit, rapetisse. Elle s'occupe sans cesse de ressemblances."[28]

One may conclude, then, that the more conservative aspects of Delacroix's conception of the imagination — his insistence that its raw material consist of known values and his rejection of fantastic, Poe-like spectacles — probably account for the nature of the subject matter treated in his art. For it is, perhaps, surprising to discover the painter to whom Baudelaire ascribed the profoundest imaginative powers of his time utilizing subject matter that has roots in nature (portraits, landscapes, still life, Moroccan studies, etc.), in literature (from the works of Goethe, Shakespeare, Byron, Scott, Tasso, etc.), in the Old and New Testaments, and in contemporary, Renaissance, Medieval, and Ancient history. That is to say, Delacroix derived his subjects from exterior sources unlike Blake and Redon who, in many of their works, explored the more fantastic reaches of the unlimited imagination.

This preoccupation with the phenomenon of the imagination

[26] De Piles, *Cours de peinture par principes*, p. 62.
[27] Quoted by Margaret Gilman, "The Poet according to Diderot," *Romanic Review*, XXXVII, p. 39. This article provides a valuable account of the history of the imagination.
[28] From Diderot's Salon of 1767; see *Œuvres complètes de Diderot*, XI, p. 131.

did not end with the consideration of its role in the genesis of the work of art; he was equally concerned with the manner in which the spectator might be invited to exercise his powers of imagination — a concern which would prove to be of momentous importance for the nature of his art, especially its sketchlike quality in his mature period.

Even his early pictures appeared novel and reprehensible in technique to many of the conservative critics who opposed his technical challenge to the smooth surfaces of David and his followers. Delécluze only repeated the opinion of other hostile writers when he accused Delacroix of an alleged inability to complete his pictures. In the *Execution of Marino Faliero* of 1826 (Fig. 23) he saw nothing but "une esquisse brillante."[29] Concerning the *Emperor Justinian Composing the Institutes* of the same year he complained that "les ouvrages de M. Delacroix . . . promettent trop, ils laissent trop à désirer."[30] Delacroix, however, persevered in his attempt to make sketchlike technique an expressive device — a visual stimulus intended to activate the spectator's imagination into creative response.

On the very same day that he recorded a walk in the forest of Champrosay where the oak tree of Antin inspired thoughts of the sublime, he noted certain ideas on the value of the sketch as compared with finished painting: ". . . l'ébauche d'un tableau, d'un monument, qu'une ruine aussi, enfin que tout ouvrage d'imagination auquel il manque des parties, doit agir davantage sur l'âme, à raison de ce que celle-ci y ajoute, tout en recueillant l'impression de cet objet."[31] Later that year, on October 26, he deplored a high degree of finish because of its tendency to limit those qualities in a work of art that stimulate the imaginative powers of the spectator: "C'est toujours l'histoire de l'ouvrage fini comparé à son ébauche . . . du monument qui ne montre que ses grands traits principaux, avant que l'achèvement et le coordonnement de toutes les parties lui aient donné quelque chose de plus arrêté et par con-

[29] From J. E. Delécluze's Salon of 1827, which appeared in the *Journal des débats* of December 20, 1827. Quoted by Lucie Horner, *Baudelaire: critique de Delacroix*, Geneva, 1956, p. 18.
[30] Also from Delécluze's Salon of 1827. Quoted by Tourneux, *Eugène Delacroix devant ses contemporains*, p. 50.
[31] *Journal*, II, pp. 41-42 (May 9, 1853).

séquent aient circonscrit l'effet sur l'imagination, laquelle se plaît au vague et se répand facilement, et embrasse de vastes objets sur des indications sommaires."[32]

However revolutionary his exploitation of sketchlike technique may have appeared to Delécluze, Delacroix was only one of a long line of writers on art who had described its advantages. The history of the reputation of the sketch is, in fact, an especially interesting one. A brief outline of its evolution will furnish a background and a context that may serve to illuminate the particular sources — de Piles, Diderot, Reynolds, La Rochefoucauld, and Lord Byron — which inspired Delacroix's conception of the sketch.

Already in the Ancient period, Pliny the Elder reported that Apelles of Kos felt he had surpassed Protogenes in painting since he knew "when to take his hand from a picture," an opinion shared by Pliny who considered this criticism "a memorable saying, showing that too much care may often be hurtful."[33] This interest in the value of unfinish appears again in Italy in the Renaissance. Alberti declared that "it is best to avoid the vitiating effect of those who wish to eliminate every weakness and make everything too polished. In their hands the work becomes old and squeezed dry before it is finished."[34] In the view of the French Academy in the seventeenth century, however, such technical freedom became suspect. André Félibien criticized the sketchy and loose quality of Rubens' pictures, attributing to the Flemish master a "grande liberté qu'il avoit à peindre," which, in Félibien's mind, "fait voir

[32] *Journal*, II, pp. 102-3 (October 26, 1853). For Delacroix, the exploitation of sketchlike technique in the finished products of the visual arts of sculpture and painting was but another mark of their superiority over literature and music in which "l'inachèvement des détails sera d'un plus grand inconvénient que dans un marbre ou un tableau; en un mot, l'à peu près y est insupportable, ou plutôt ce qu'on appelle, en peinture, l'*indication*, le *croquis*, y est impossible . . ." *Journal*, II, p. 159 (April 4, 1854).

[33] K. Jex-Blake and E. Sellers, *The Elder Pliny's Chapters on the History of Art*, London, 1896, Bk. xxxv, pp. 120-21. "Et aliam gloriam usurpavit [Apelles], cum Protogenis opus inmensi laboris ac curae supra modum anxiae miraretur, dixit enim omnia sibi cum illo paria esse aut illi meliora, sed uno se praestare, quod manim de tabula sciret tollere, memorabili praecepto nocere saepe nimiam diligentiam."

[34] Alberti, *On Painting*, p. 97. He also cites the example of Protogenes who "did not know how to raise his hand from his panel." *Loc.cit.* For Michelangelo's conception of the role of lack of finish in art see Robert J. Clements, "Michelangelo on Effort and Rapidity in Art," *Journal of the Warburg and Courtauld Institutes*, XVII (1954), pp. 301-10.

en plusieurs de ses tableaux plus de pratique de pinceau, que de correction dans les choses où la nature doit estre exactement représentée, non seulement dans son dessein, mais aussi dans son coloris, où les teintes des carnations paroissent souvent si fortes et si séparées les unes des autres, qu'elles semblent des taches. . . ."[35] The anti-sketch position became one of the rallying points of French Classicism in other fields as well. Boileau, in *L'Art poétique*, prescribed for literature a mode of artistic creation that would culminate in a highly finished work:

> Hâtez-vous lentement; et, sans perdre courage,
> Vingt fois sur le métier remettez votre ouvrage:
> Polissez-le sans cesse et le repolissez;
> Ajoutez quelquefois, et souvent effacez.[36]

Nevertheless, it was an author of the seventeenth century who provided Delacroix one of his sources for a pro-sketch statement. On June 29, 1857, he noted in the Journal[37] the 627th maxim of La Rochefoucauld, which states: "Il y a de belles choses qui ont plus d'éclat quand elles demeurent imparfaites, que quand elles sont trop achevées."[38] Indicative of his ability to range freely in the realm of art theory is the reminder following this quotation that this passage was intended (probably in the projected *Dictionnaire*) "pour aller avec ce que Lord Byron dit du poète Campbell qu'il finit trop ses ouvrages." Delacroix had, in fact, on July 15, 1850,[39] transcribed a lengthy quotation from Captain T. Medwin's *Journal of the Conversations of Lord Byron*, which provided contemporary authority from one of his favorite poets for La Rochefoucauld's assertion that lack of finish produced greater brilliance of effect. According to Captain Medwin, Byron had asserted (in the French translation) that "les poésies de Campbell[40] . . . sentent trop

[35] Félibien, *Entretiens sur les vies et sur les ouvrages des plus excellens peintres*, II, p. 214.
[36] *Œuvres complètes de Boileau-Despréaux*, p. 244.
[37] *Journal*, III, pp. 108-9 (June 29, 1857).
[38] François de la Rochefoucauld, *Œuvres complètes*, ed. L. Martin-Chauffier, Argenteuil, 1935, p. 347. Here it appears among the "maximes supprimées." According to E. B. O. Borgerhoff (*The Freedom of French Classicism*, Princeton, 1950, p. 108), maxim 627 appeared only in the edition of 1665 of La Rochefoucauld's works, after which it was deleted.
[39] *Journal*, I, p. 388.
[40] Thomas Campbell (1773-1844), the Scottish poet.

la lampe. Il n'est jamais content de ce qu'il fait. Il a gâté ses plus belles productions en voulant trop les finir. Tout le brillant du premier jet est perdu. Il en est des poèmes commes des tableaux. Ils ne doivent pas être trop finis. Le grand art est l'effet, n'importe comment on le produit."[41]

So far, however, art theorists had advocated lack of finish in order to avoid dryness, in order to achieve spontaneity or brilliance of effect. For the impact of the sketch upon the imagination we must seek elsewhere for Delacroix's sources.

Roger de Piles, in his *Conversations sur la peinture*, which appeared in the *Recueil de divers ouvrages sur la peinture et le coloris*, a work that Delacroix knew,[42] had introduced the concept of the imagination into the discussion of the sketch. One of the two participants in the conversation, Pamphile, remarks that "les ouvrages les plus finis . . . ne sont pas toujours les plus agréables; et les tableaux artistement touchés font le même effet qu'un discours, où les choses n'étant pas expliquées avec toutes leurs circonstances, en laissent juger le lecteur, qui se fait un plaisir d'imaginer tout ce que l'auteur avoit dans l'esprit."[43] Significantly, because of Delacroix's well-known penchant for Rubensian technique, Pamphile, in this passage, had been defending Rubens against the charge that it was the Flemish painter's fiery genius which prevented him from achieving the required finish in his pictures.

The power of the sketch to stimulate the imagination of the spectator became a widespread notion and, surprisingly, appears even in the predominantly Classical theory of the Comte de Caylus, who

[41] Captain Medwin's English reads: "Like Gray," said he [Byron], "Campbell smells too much of the oil: he is never satisfied with what he does, his finest things have been spoiled by over-polish — the sharpness of the outline is worn off. Like paintings, poems may be too highly finished. The great art is effect, no matter how produced." Thomas Medwin, *The Journal of the Conversations of Lord Byron*, New York, 1824, pp. 73-74. According to George Heard Hamilton ("Eugène Delacroix and Lord Byron," *Gazette des Beaux-Arts*, February 1943, pp. 99-110, and *ibid.*, July-December 1944, pp. 365-86), Delacroix utilized Amadée Pichot's translation of the works of Byron, *Œuvres complètes de Lord Byron*, 4th ed., Paris, 1822-25. This included a translation of Medwin's Journal. For French translations of Byron's works, see Edmond Estève, *Byron et le romantisme français*, Paris, 1907, pp. 526-33.

[42] See above pp. 75-76 and nn. 17, 18.

[43] De Piles, *Recueil de divers ouvrages sur la peinture et le coloris*, p. 62.

declared in a discourse presented to the Academy in 1732: "Il me semble qu'un simple trait déterminant souvent une passion et prouvant combien l'Esprit de l'auteur ressentoit alors la force et la vérité de l'expression; l'œil curieux et l'imagination animée se plaisent et sont flattés d'achever ce qui souvent n'est qu'ébauché."[44]

It is no wonder, then, that the idea appears again in the Proto-Romantic theory of Diderot who contributes a new element by emphasizing the liberating influence of the sketch upon the imagination. For while de Piles and the Comte de Caylus had limited the achievement of the stimulated imagination of the spectator to the original inspiration of the artist, Diderot permits the imagination to use the sketch as a springboard for original and creative thought: "L'esquisse," he claims, "ne nous attache peut-être si fort, que parce qu'étant indéterminée, elle laisse plus de liberté à notre imagination, qui y voit tout ce qu'il lui plaît."[45]

Across the Channel, Sir Joshua Reynolds, Delacroix's favorite English theorist,[46] eloquently expounded a similar conception of the relation of the sketch and the imagination. In his view, the imagination played a primary role in art for he declares, in his Fourth Discourse, of December 10, 1771, that "the great end of the art is to strike the imagination."[47] And, elsewhere, he suggested that a finished work might appear to the spectator less appealing than its sketch, which possessed special evocative powers: "It is true, sketches, or such drawings as painters usually make for their works, give this pleasure of the imagination to a high degree. From a

---

[44] This discourse was delivered to the Academy June 7, 1732, by the Comte de Caylus. Entitled "Discours du Comte de Caylus sur les dessins," it was published in the *Revue universelle des arts*, IX (1859), pp. 314-23, whence I have derived the cited passage (p. 318). In 1745, a similar notion was advanced by A. J. Dezallier d'Argenville in *Abrégé de la vie des plus fameux peintres*, Paris, 1745, I, pp. xxxj-xxxij: "Les grands maîtres finissent peu leurs desseins, ils se contentent de faire des esquisses, ou griffonnemens faits de rien, qui ne plaisent pas aux demi-connoisseurs, ils veulent quelque chose de terminé qui soit agréable aux yeux: un vrai connoisseur pense autrement; il voit dans un croquis la manière de penser d'un grand maître pour caractériser chaque objet avec peu de traits; son imagination animée par le beau feu qui régne dans le dessein perce à travers ce qui y manque, elle apperçoit souvent ce qui n'y est pas et ce qui y doit être."

[45] From Diderot's Salon of 1767; see *Œuvres complètes de Diderot*, XI, p. 246.

[46] See the *Supplément* of the *Journal*, III, pp. 358-59, in which Delacroix liberally cites Reynolds in the preparatory notes for his article on Raphael.

[47] *Sir Joshua Reynolds: Discourses on Art*, p. 59.

slight undetermined drawing, where the ideas of the composition and character are, as I may say, only just touched upon, the imagination supplies more than the painter himself, probably, could produce; and we accordingly often find that the finished work disappoints the expectation that was raised from the sketch. . . ."[48]

Therefore, Delécluze's criticism of the sketchlike quality of Delacroix's finished paintings disregards the existence of theoretical tradition, which provides ample justification for this particular technique. Of course, he was unaware that Delacroix had availed himself of the two traditional arguments for the lack of finish: high finish or polish as depriving the finished work of brilliance of effect and the power of the sketch to stimulate the imagination, especially the concept of the liberation of the spectator's imagination beyond the original conception of the artist.

Delacroix's interest in the special properties of the sketch derived, no doubt, from his dissatisfaction with the Davidian tradition that considered perfection of finish as one of the basic ingredients of the Neo-Classical style. Ingres, Delacroix's arch-foe, in this matter, had once declared that "il faut faire disparaître les traces de la facilité; ce sont les résultats et non les moyens employés qui doivent paraître. . . ."[49] No wonder Delacroix once complained that Ingres possessed "point d'imagination,"[50] for his paintings demonstrate an ever-increasing exploitation of a sketchlike technique which culminates in late works such as *Tobias and the Angel* of 1863 (Fig. 24) where linear precision and discreet brushwork, both hallmarks of Neo-Classical technique, are obliterated by the free, broad application of pigment. Precise detail and smooth surfaces disappear and, in their place, a rapid, summary, almost autonomous network of brushstrokes creates a brilliant, agitated entity which, alone, conveys an adequate expression of Delacroix's impassioned rejection of Neo-Classical vision.

The shock value of this revolution in technique for his contemporary critics may strike the sophisticated spectator of the twentieth century as difficult to grasp in view of Impressionist, Post-Impres-

[48] *Ibid.*, pp. 163-64. This passage is from the Eighth Discourse of December 10, 1778.
[49] Jean Auguste Dominique Ingres, *Écrits sur l'art*, Paris, 1947, p. 14.
[50] *Journal*, II, p. 153 (March 24, 1854).

sionist, and modern indulgence in sketchlike effects. However, to a Neo-Classic critic like Delécluze, even the early *Marino Faliero* of 1826 (Fig. 23) was open to question. And, indeed, its disregard of precise rendering of minute detail, flat rendering of color areas, and rejection of linear emphasis must have appeared novel and sketch-like. Hence, his characterization of it as "une esquisse brillante."

To the modern spectator, the nature of the technique in this early work suggests that Delacroix, in the 1820's, utilized lack of detail and a broad brushstroke in order to obtain the result de-scribed by La Rochefoucauld and Byron: a heightened measure of sensuous brilliance. It is quite appropriate in this particular case since the subject matter is Venetian. Moreover, we know that he admired the brilliant color effects of Veronese and Titian.[51]

Nevertheless, in the 1820's (witness such examples as *Dante and Virgil, Massacre at Chios,* and *Death of Sardanapalus*), he did not yet attempt to render in a finished work the vibrancy, spontaneity, and visual ambiguity inherent in the sketch. There is nothing visually ambiguous in the *Marino Faliero.* If each detail lacks precision of rendering, the general characteristics of each object do retain identity. In the 1830's, certain works, especially *Boissy d'Anglas at the Convention* of 1831 (Fig. 25), display a loosening of technique but it was not until the 1840's that the exploitation of unfinish became a dominant characteristic of his style. Thus he anticipated in practice what was to be formulated in theory in the 1850's — the stimulation of the responsive imagination by a pro-vocatively unfinished technique. In *St. George and the Dragon* of 1847 (Fig. 26) brushwork has become entirely negligent of descrip-tive detail; faces are summarily indicated; boundaries of individual objects and figures have been violated by active brushstrokes, so that objects tend to lose their linear identity and to become fused in the agitated surface of paint. Furthermore, ample areas of im-penetrable gloom contribute to the suggestive power of this pic-ture, which exemplifies Delacroix's belief that an unfinished qual-ity would appeal to "l'imagination, laquelle se plaît au vague et se

51 See pp. 57-60 of the *Journal,* III, for extensive analysis of the art of these two Venetian masters. See René Huyghe, *Delacroix,* p. 204, for the relation of this picture with the art of Bonington.

répand facilement, et embrasse de vastes objets sur des indications sommaires."[52]

And yet, the fact remains that his finished pictures never approached the complete freedom of visual expression evident in his sketches. Consider the painted sketch for the *Lion Hunt* of 1855 (Fig. 27). It brings to mind Delacroix's prophetic statement that painting need not always have a subject.[53] The entangled mass of men, animals, and weapons has been rendered with such broad, summary treatment that the precise nature of the action and the role of the combatants have been submerged. Swirling, vibrant strokes of the brush have taken precedence so that the main effect resembles an abstract expression of the physical and psychical action involved in this tumultuous theme. On the other hand, the finished picture (Fig. 28; half destroyed by fire in 1870)[54] departs appreciably from the freedom of brush in the direction of a relatively literal, tight rendering of the scene. The figures and animals here receive a vibrant and pulsating treatment, to be sure. Nevertheless, the brushstrokes also describe the tone and texture of specific objects, leaving less for the imagination to supply.

The question arises: Why did Delacroix, in his finished pictures, never abandon himself to the absolute freedom of the sketch, which, with its power to stimulate the imagination, obviously presented an admirable solution to the problem of Romantic expression? The answer lies in his characteristic ability to appreciate the advantages of contrasting approaches to art. In 1853, in the very act of demonstrating the value of the sketch, he conceded that finish as opposed to sketchiness afforded the painter unique advantages. While granting "l'effet immanquable de l'ébauche comparée au tableau fini, qui est toujours un peu gâté quant à la touche," he nevertheless held in good regard the finished work "dans lequel

[52] *Journal*, II, pp. 102-3 (October 26, 1853).

[53] "La peinture n'a pas toujours besoin d'un sujet." *Journal*, III, p. 24 (January 13, 1857).

[54] A small replica of this picture in a private collection (illustrated in Jean Cassou, *Delacroix*, Paris, 1947, pl. 34) indicates the nature of the lost section of the completed picture. The Louvre possesses a pencil study for the left part of the picture; see the catalogue of the centenary exhibition, *Centenaire d'Eugène Delacroix: 1798-1863*, Paris, 1963, no. 467.

l'harmonie et la profondeur des expressions deviennent une compensation."[55]

In this matter it is well to point out that his pictures were rarely the product of one, swift campaign before the easel under the inspiration of the moment. Rather, he adhered to the traditional, Academic method of a reasoned and measured solution of pictorial problems by means of preparatory work. The preparatory sketch for the *Lion Hunt* is but one example. After his death, the executors of his estate discovered more than six thousand drawings in various media.[56] In writing, he confirmed this practice suggesting that while "l'exécution, dans la peinture, doit toujours tenir de l'improvisation,"[57] a rational and critical development of the original engendered a higher degree of "harmonie et la profondeur des expressions." In this respect, he once again echoed Diderot, who had indicated the different factors that should control the sketch and the finished product, proclaiming: "Une bonne esquisse peut être la production d'un jeune homme plein de verve et de feu, que rien ne captive, qui s'abandonne à sa fougue. Un bon tableau n'est jamais que l'œuvre d'un maître qui a beaucoup réfléchi, médité, travaillé."[58]

One can discern, then, in Delacroix's conception of the sketch and the finished painting a characteristic ability to appreciate both sides of the coin. Relying upon the authority of La Rochefoucauld, Byron, Roger de Piles, Diderot, and Reynolds, he felt free to seek in his pictures a varying degree of unfinish, both for greater brilliance and for imaginative stimulation; as a result, he liberated painting from the tight, polished surfaces of the schools of David and Ingres in the interests of subjective expression. Yet, true to the

---

[55] *Journal*, II, p. 58 (May 21, 1853).

[56] According to Philippe Burty, ed., *Lettres de Eugène Delacroix*, Paris, 1878, p. x. Burty also asserts that "il voulait qu'après sa mort, ils [his drawings] vinssent, comme un argument solonnel, protester contre les reproches amers d'improvisation et de facilité dont on l'avait poursuivi, et prouver qu'une 'improvisation' aussi abondante et aussi solide que celle dont il avait fait preuve dans ses travaux décoratifs et ses tableaux, qu'une semblable facilité à exprimer le sentiment et l'idée, à adapter l'esprit du dessin et de la couleur aux convenances du sujet choisi, eussent été, sans le secours préalable de l'étude la plus persistante et la plus méthodique, des phénomènes sans exemples dans l'histoire de l'art." *Ibid.*, p. xi.

[57] *Journal*, I, p. 174 (January 27, 1847).

[58] From Diderot's Salon of 1767; see *Œuvres complètes de Diderot*, XI, p. 322.

national genius, he retained traditional control in the finished product in the belief that greater harmony and profundity provided compensatory values.

The fundamental importance of the rational process in Delacroix's conception of creativity also finds expression in his definition of genius. The characteristic Romantic notion of the irrationally inspired genius had advocates in eighteenth-century England. Edward Young, in *Conjectures on Original Composition* of 1759, had defined the irrational nature of this essential endowment, which he attributed to the intervention of divine favor: "Learning we thank, genius we revere; that gives us pleasure, this gives us rapture; that informs, this inspires; and is itself inspired; for genius is from heaven; learning from man."[59] Delacroix, however, preferred to temper this conception by way of including the inhibitory ingredient of rational control. For his part, he had little patience with contemporary painters, writers, and musicians who justified extravagant licenses in art and life by a claim to original genius. He referred to them as "de prétendus hommes de génie comme nous en voyons aujourd'hui, remplis d'affectation et de ridicule, chez lesquels le mauvais goût le dispute à la prétention, dont l'idée est toujours obscurcie par des nuages, qui portent, même dans leur conduite, cette bizarrerie qu'ils croient un signe de talent, sont des fantômes d'écrivains, de peintres et de musiciens."[60] In personal conduct, of course, Delacroix was noted for aristocratic and gentlemanly bearing and in art he demanded a similar rational restraint. So we are not surprised to discover that his definition of genius makes reason its dominant feature. "Le plus grand génie n'est qu'un être supérieurement raisonnable," he wrote in 1855;[61] and elsewhere he noted that in such favorite masters as Mozart, Molière, and Racine, reason amounted to the primary element of their genius: "Mozart, ni Molière, ni Racine ne devaient avoir de sottes préférences, ni de sottes antipathies; leur *raison*, par con-

[59] Edward Young, "Conjectures on Original Composition," *The Works of the Author of the Night-Thoughts,* London, 1773, v, pp. 102-3.
[60] *Journal,* II, p. 371 (August 31, 1855).
[61] *Ibid.,* pp. 371-72.

séquent, était à la hauteur de leur *génie,* ou plutôt était *leur génie même."*[62]

Numerous art theorists whose works were known to Delacroix had voiced opposition to free indulgence in the inspiration characteristic of genius. Even Longinus, who otherwise linked the attainment of the sublime with the operation of genius, declared that "genius needs the curb as often as the spur."[63] De Piles, while admitting that "le Génie est la première chose que l'on doit supposer dans un Peintre,"[64] still held that it alone was not sufficient for the production of an enduring work of art. "Il faut donc du Génie," he granted, "mais un Génie éxercé par les règles, par les réfléxions, et par l'assiduité du travail. Il faut avoir beaucoup vû, beaucoup lû et beaucoup étudié pour diriger ce Génie, et pour le rendre capable de produire des choses dignes de la postérité."[65]

The portrayal of the unbridled imagination as a dangerous principle without some degree of rational moderation was the essential theme of Diderot's *Paradoxe sur le comédien,* which Delacroix knew.[66] Therein, Diderot maintained that both inspiration and judgment are required in the actor's art: "C'est lorsque, suspendus entre la nature et leur ébauche, ces génies portent alternativement un œil attentif sur l'une et l'autre; les beautés d'inspiration, les traits fortuits qu'ils répandent dans leurs ouvrages, et dont l'apparition subite les étonne eux-mêmes, sont d'un effet et d'un succès bien autrement assurés que ce qu'ils y ont jeté de boutade. C'est au sang-froid à tempérer le délire de l'enthousiasme." And the speaker of this argument develops his theme in terms that anticipate Delacroix's distaste for the irrational and eccentric spirits of his age. "Ce n'est pas l'homme violent qui est hors de lui-même qui dispose de nous," he suggests; rather, "c'est un avantage réservé à l'homme qui se possède. Les grands poëtes dramatiques surtout sont spectateurs assidus de ce qui se passe autour d'eux dans le monde physique et dans le monde moral."[67]

[62] *Ibid.,* p. 318 (March 15, 1855). The italics are Delacroix's.
[63] Longinus, *On the Sublime,* p. 127.
[64] De Piles, *Abrégé de la vie des peintres,* p. 1.
[65] *Ibid.,* p. 14.
[66] On January 27, 1847, Delacroix, inspired by a recent discussion of Diderot's work at a social gathering, devotes a lengthy passage in the Journal to a comparison of the arts of painting and of acting. *Journal,* I, pp. 170-74.
[67] Denis Diderot, "Paradoxe sur le comédien," *Œuvres complètes de Diderot,*

It is tempting to surmise that another element of the traditional conception of genius was in part responsible for Delacroix's aversion to art schools and academies as well as his reluctance to found a school of his own. We have already noted his hostile attitude towards the Academy, which fostered, in his opinion, a tendency to stifle the student's imagination in favor of sterile copying of fashionable old masters.[68] Apart from this, however, his personal disinclination to found a school[69] must have been influenced by the venerable notion that genius simply could not be taught.

Already in the seventeenth century literary theory had endowed genius with the power to suggest mysterious and irrational qualities by means of art — qualities, furthermore, that were described as untransmittable by precept to students. Rapin, for example, proclaimed, in his *Réflexions sur la poétique*, that "il y a encore dans la poésie comme dans les autres arts de certaines choses ineffables, et qu'on ne peut expliquer: ces choses sont comme des mystères. Il n'y a point de préceptes pour enseigner ces grâces secrètes, ces charmes imperceptibles et tous ces agréments cachés de la poésie qui vont au cœur."[70] Later, de Piles echoed this sentiment with special emphasis on the conception of genius as a mysterious gift, incapable of translation into precepts of study: "Le Génie est la première chose que l'on doit supposer dans un Peintre.

VIII, p. 367. In this matter it is worth noting the opinion of Immanuel Kant, who played such an important role in the formulation of Romantic aesthetics, whose ideas were popularized by Madame de Staël, and whose works were available in France in translation at an early period (see M. Vallois, *La formation de l'influence Kantienne en France*, Paris, n.d., esp. pp. 46-47). He, too, conforms to the traditional conception of the necessity of rational restraint of the dictates of genius: "Genius can only furnish rich *material* for products of beautiful art; its execution and its *form* require talent cultivated in the schools, in order to make such a use of the material as will stand examination by the Judgement." *Kant's Critique of Judgment*, tr. J. H. Bernard, London, 1914, p. 193.

[68] This hostility is evident in the sarcastic passage entered in the Journal on November 25, 1855: "Tirer de son imagination des moyens de rendre la nature et ses effets, et les rendre suivant son tempérament propre: chimères, étude vaine que ne donnent ni le prix de Rome, ni l'Institut; copier l'exécution du Guide ou celle de Raphaël, suivant la mode." *Journal*, II, p. 414.

[69] In a letter of June 8, 1855 (Joubin's date), he declared that "les écoles, les coteries ne sont autre chose que des associations de médiocrités, pour se garantir mutuellement un semblant de renommée qui à la vérité est de courte durée mais qui fait traverser la vie agréablement." *Correspondance générale*, III, p. 265.

[70] R. Rapin, "Réflexions sur la poétique," *Œuvres*, The Hague, 1725, II, p. 130; quoted by Borgerhoff, *The Freedom of French Classicism*, pp. 181-82.

C'est une partie qui ne peut s'aquérir ni par l'étude; ni par le travail. . . ."[71]

For Delacroix the most stimulating discussion of this problem occurred, no doubt, in the pages of the *Spectator*. In the Journal entry of October 26, 1853, he cites Addison on this topic and develops a lengthy discussion. "Le *Spectateur*," he observes, "parle de ce qu'il appelle *génies de premier ordre*, tels que Pindare, Homère, la Bible, — confus au milieu de choses sublimes et inachevées, — Shakespeare, etc.; puis de ceux dans lesquels il voit plus d'art, tels que Virgile, Platon, etc. . . ."[72] This conception derives from the *Spectator* paper of September 3, 1711, in which Addison had stated his well-known distinction between first-class and second-class geniuses. The first category, which includes Homer, comprises those "great natural Genius's that were never disciplined and broken by Rules of Art,"[73] while the second category comprised "those that have formed themselves by Rules, and submitted the Greatness of their natural Talents to the Corrections and Restraints of Art."[74]

Especially noteworthy is Addison's desire to admonish those lesser poets of restricted imagination who would dare to emulate the privileged way of geniuses of the first class. "I cannot," he sternly remarks, "quit this Head without observing that *Pindar* was a great Genius of the first Class, who was hurried on by a Natural Fire and Impetuosity to vast Conceptions of things, and noble Sallies of Imagination. At the same time, can anything be more ridiculous than for Men of a sober and moderate Fancy to imitate this Poet's Way of Writing in those monstrous Compositions which go among us under the Name of Pindaricks?"[75] Delacroix, in his commentary on this passage, adopts the view that geniuses of the undisciplined type afford dangerous examples for study to eager admirers. "Si des génies tels que les Homère et les Shakespeare offrent des côtés si désagréables, que sera-ce des imitateurs de ce genre, abandonnés et sans précision? Le *Spectateur* les tance avec raison, et rien n'est plus détestable; c'est de tous les genres d'imitation le plus sot et le plus

---

[71] De Piles, *op.cit.*, p. 1.   [72] *Journal*, ii, p. 102.
[73] Addison and Steele, *The Spectator*, i, Vol. 2, p. 283.
[74] *Ibid.*, p. 285.   [75] *Ibid.*, p. 284.

maladroit."[76] This passage is followed by a warning to all those who would hope to emulate such formidable masters: "Rien n'est plus dangereux que ces sortes de confusions pour les jeunes esprits, toujours portés à admirer ce qui est gigantesque plus que ce qui est raisonnable. Une manière boursouflée et incorrecte leur paraît le comble du génie, et rien n'est plus facile que l'imitation d'une semblable manière."[77]

For his own part, Delacroix, even as a youth, had felt qualified to emulate the most unequal and disheveled of painterly geniuses, namely Michelangelo and Rubens, and, no doubt, considered himself to be a genius. For although he constantly endeavored to adjust the irrational aspects of his creative gift to the restraint of reason — thereby qualifying for the title of both first-class and second-class genius according to Addisonian terminology — he regarded the nature of his own creative work to be such that it was useless to attempt to transmit it to a school of young followers.[78]

Yet another traditional aspect of genius colored his conception — the customary attribution of justifiable faults to the fiery type and a more consistent perfection to the cooler, more rational variety. He held the view that Michelangelo, Corneille, and Shakespeare were to be allowed faults and lapses in style and inspiration because of the compensating heights they attained in artistic expression. More restrained creators such as Virgil and Racine maintained, on the other hand, a steady and even flow of unblemished art: "Ceux de la seconde classe tiennent en bride leur imagination, ils se réforment ou se dirigent à leur gré, sans tomber dans des contradictions ou des erreurs choquantes."[79]

The comparison of Shakespeare as the undisciplined genius and Racine as the more rational one depends on a widespread use of these two writers as exponents of the two opposed modes of creation during the eighteenth century. Voltaire, for example, in his *Questions sur l'Encyclopédie* (which Delacroix knew) referred to

[76] *Journal*, II, p. 103 (October 26, 1853).
[77] *Ibid.*, pp. 103-4.
[78] Nevertheless, Delacroix, probably because of the aid required for the execution of the monumental works in public buildings in Paris, trained a select number of pupils and assistants, notably Pierre Andrieu, Gustave Lassalle-Bordes, and Louis de Planet. See Escholier, *Delacroix: peintre, graveur, écrivain*, III, for the role played by these and other assistants in these works.
[79] *Journal*, II, p. 456 (June 10, 1856).

Shakespeare as the more natural artist in whose works "c'est la vérité, c'est la nature elle-même qui parle son propre langage sans aucun mélange de l'art."[80] Racine, on the other hand, whom he endowed with the eighteenth-century attribute of taste, never fell into error: "Le génie conduit par le goût ne sera jamais de faute grossière, aussi *Racine* depuis *Andromaque*, le *Poussin, Rameau* n'en ont jamais fait."[81]

It is in the context of the hostile reaction that often greeted his pictures that this preoccupation with the nature of genius takes on particular significance. In the traditional conception of justifiable lapses from correctness for the type of genius represented by Homer, Shakespeare, and Corneille, Delacroix must have found solace to ease the discouraging attacks of critics such as Guyot de Fère, who in 1835 announced: "M. Delacroix, à ce qu'il nous semble, va toujours *decrescendo*, que dire de sa pochade du *Prisonnier de Chillon* où tant d'incorrections se font sentir?"[82]

The license traditionally accorded the genius had other ramifications for Delacroix's thought. For a Romantic painter the validity of Academic rules was an especially sensitive subject. Here, too, his position is one that avoids iconoclasm and rash rejection of all restraints.

RULES

Previous art theory had condoned in the genius not only faulty expression but also a corresponding release from the customary dictates of Academic rules. Roger de Piles was one of those who described the freedom allowed in such cases: " . . . vous sçavez qu'il y a des génies assez heureux pour apprendre toutes choses sans autres règles que celle de leur bon sens, avec une certaine lumière naturelle qui leur fait suivre ce qui est bien, et fuir ce qui est mal."[83] This liberality of viewpoint towards rules found welcome support in England where critics had never felt comfortable under the imposition of Academic precepts imported from France as exemplified in the theory of Dryden. Addison turned to an ancient author, Longinus, as an authoritative source for the antirational

---

[80] Voltaire, *Questions sur l'Encyclopédie par des amateurs*, I, Part II, p. 142.
[81] *Ibid.*, II, Part VI, p. 182.
[82] Quoted by Tourneux, *Eugène Delacroix devant ses contemporains*, p. 62.
[83] De Piles, *Dialogue sur le coloris*, pp. 41-42.

tendencies eighteenth-century criticism would soon take. "I must also observe with *Longinus*," he wrote, "that the Productions of a great Genius, with many Lapses and Inadvertencies, are infinitely preferable to the works of an inferior kind of Author, which are scrupulously exact and conformable to all the Rules of correct Writing."[84] Not much later, a similar tendency appeared in France. Diderot, in his *Pensées détachées*, advised the use of rules only for very ordinary individuals and deplored the debilitating effect of rules on art: "Les règles ont fait de l'art une routine; et je ne sais si elles n'ont pas été plus nuisibles qu'utiles. Entendons-nous: elles ont servi à l'homme ordinaire; elles ont nui à l'homme de génie."[85]

Romantic aesthetics, which generally sought to free the artist from restraint of any kind, inevitably adopted and intensified this opposition to creation according to prescribed formulae. Madame de Staël, for example, dismissed rules as fit only for rank beginners claiming that "ces règles ne sont que des barrières pour empêcher les enfants de tomber."[86] Delacroix, however, characteristically sought authority in Classical sources for this liberal position.

Distaste for rules is evident in the approval he accorded a statement of one of his friends, Abel-Jean-Henri Dufresne.[87] In 1824, during his youth, when dissatisfaction with Academic rule was naturally quite strong, he recorded in the Journal Dufresne's attitude: "Dufresne dit une chose fort juste: que ce qui faisait l'homme extraordinaire était, radicalement, une manière tout à fait propre à lui de voir les choses. Il l'étendait aux grands capitaines, etc., enfin aux grands esprits de tous les genres. Ainsi, point de règles pour les grandes âmes; elles sont pour les gens qui n'ont que le talent qu'on acquiert."[88]

---

[84] Addison and Steele, *The Spectator*, II, Vol. 4, p. 154; from paper 291 of February 2, 1712. Opposition to French criteria was voiced by Edward Filmer: "These *Corneillean* Rules are as Dissonant to the *English* Constitution of the Stage, as the *French* Slavery to our *English* liberty." Edward Filmer, *Defense of Dramatic Poetry* (1698), II, p. 28; quoted by Walter Jackson Bate, *From Classic to Romantic*, New York, 1961, p. 46.

[85] Diderot, *Essais sur la peinture*, p. 121.

[86] De Staël, *De l'Allemagne*, p. 482.

[87] Abel-Jean-Henri Dufresne (1788-1862) was a versatile personality active as magistrate, writer, and painter. A student of Watelet, he first exhibited in the Salon of 1817.

[88] *Journal*, I, p. 87 (March 27, 1824). Both Lucien Rudrauf, *Delacroix et le problème du romantisme artistique*, p. 285, and Hubert Gillot, *E. Delacroix:*

The part rules played in the creative process had been one of the most controversial issues involved in the battle of the Ancients versus the Moderns that had raged in the seventeenth and eighteenth centuries.[89] It is from writers of this vintage that Delacroix culled authority for the liberal interpretation of this problem. In 1855, for example, he copied from M. Bret's *Supplément à la vie de Molière* an account of that playwright's refusal to alter a few words of *Tartuffe* for the purpose of stricter adherence to more perfect rhyme forms: "Molière soutint qu'il fallait s'en tenir à la première expression et que la raison et l'art même demandaient et autorisaient souvent le sacrifice d'une plus grande perfection des vers à une plus grande justesse."[90] Worth noting is the fact that this passage also cites Boileau's liberal interpretation of rules in the fourth book of *L'Art poétique*:

> Quelquefois dans sa course un esprit vigoureux
> Trop resserré par l'art sort des règles prescrites,
> Et de l'art même apprend à franchir les limites.[91]

That freedom from tyranny of rules implicit even in French Classical theory was congenial to Delacroix is evident in the comment he makes on this matter: "Je suis ravi pour ma part de cet exemple: Molière est ici évidemment plus grand artiste que Racine qui ne se montre qu'homme de métier."[92] And in the works of Montesquieu he found further justification for freedom from rule for the outstanding individual — one might correctly say the genius. "Montesquieu dit très bien," he remarked, "*qu'un homme qui écrit bien n'écrit pas comme on écrit, mais comme il écrit,* c'est-à-dire comme il pense."[93] This notion of Montesquieu, which is derived from his *Pensées diverses*,[94] he underscored precisely in that

---

l'homme, ses idées, son œuvre, p. 270, misrepresent the last sentence of this passage as Delacroix's own assertion. Actually it is a part of his paraphrase of Dufresne's argument — which, to be sure, he approves.

[89] See above, p. 17, n. 21, for bibliography on this subject.

[90] *Journal*, II, p. 358 (July 17, 1855). Delacroix included in this entry a number of quotations derived from M. Bret, "Supplément à la vie de Molière," *Œuvres de Molière*, ed. M. Bret, I, Paris, 1804. The cited quotation is from p. 55.

[91] Bret, *op.cit.*, p. 56.   [92] *Journal*, II, p. 359.   [93] *Ibid.*

[94] Charles Louis de Secondat Montesquieu, "Pensées diverses," *Œuvres complètes de Montesquieu*, Paris, 1823, V, p. 236. The complete passage reads: "Un homme qui écrit bien n'écrit pas comme on écrit, mais comme il écrit; et c'est souvent en parlant mal qu'il parle bien."

part which declares the sanctity of freedom of expression dear to every Romantic artist.

So, once more the curious mixture of iconoclasm and traditionalism appears in Delacroix's thought. While exalting the principle of Romantic license in regard to the rules, he nevertheless turned to various non-Romantic sources in order to justify this course, thus displaying the innate and consistent conservatism which always tempered his Romantic fire.

BOLDNESS

Another aspect of the creative process which can be described as fundamentally Romantic was *hardiesse* or boldness — a quality that found an ardent advocate in Delacroix, who ascribed much of Rubens' impact to its presence in his art. "En se permettant tout, il [Rubens] vous porte au delà de la limite qu'atteignent à peine les plus grands peintres; il vous domine, il vous écrase sous tant de liberté et de hardiesse."[95]

Traditionally, boldness had long been cited as one of the requisite attributes of genius. Sir Joshua Reynolds, for example, had, on condition that a solid foundation in knowledge of the old masters be observed, advised its cultivation, suggesting that "when an Artist is sure that he is upon firm ground, supported by the authority and practice of his predecessors of the greatest reputation, he may then assume the boldness and intrepidity of genius."[96]

Delacroix shared Reynolds' belief in the need for a solid foundation for the bold flights of genius citing experience as the indispensable basis: "L'expérience est indispensable pour apprendre tout ce qu'on peut faire avec son instrument. . . ."[97] Yet (and it is worth noting the existence of this strong element of Romantic enthusiasm in the mature artist of 1850) he emphatically endorses the bold attack on artistic problems: "Et pourtant il faut être très hardi! Sans hardiesse et une hardiesse extrême, il n'y a pas de beautés."[98]

Boldness and enthusiasm, however, were not to be maintained

[95] *Journal*, III, pp. 307-8 (October 21, 1860).
[96] *Sir Joshua Reynolds: Discourses on Art*, p. 90; from the Fifth Discourse of December 10, 1772.
[97] *Journal*, I, p. 393 (July 21, 1850).   [98] *Ibid.*, p. 394.

with the aid of artificial stimulants à la De Quincey. Nineteenth-century experiments with intoxicants and drugs in order to induce creative energy were rejected by the surprisingly proper leader of the Romantic Movement in painting. He harbored no sympathy for Byron's indulgence in gin. He records in the Journal his conversation with Jenny Le Guillou, his faithful servant and confidante, concerning Byron's advocacy of gin as an aid to the Muses. "Jenny me disait, quand je lui lisais ce passage de Lord Byron, où il vante le genièvre comme son Hippocrène, que c'était à cause de la hardiesse qu'il y puisait."[99] This reference derives from Thomas Medwin's *Journal of the Conversations of Lord Byron* wherein Medwin reports that the poet had suggested "humorously enough" the following words of advice: "Why don't you drink, Medwin? Gin-and-water is the source of all my inspiration. If you were to drink as much as I do, you would write as good verses: depend on it, it is the true Hippocrene."[100]

The canny insight of his untutored but shrewd servant met with her master's approval. Intoxicants, he surmised, were the probable source of boldness of spirit that enabled many artists to attain otherwise inaccessible heights. "Je crois que l'observation [of Jenny] est juste, tout humiliante qu'elle est pour un grand nombre de beaux esprits, qui ont trouvé dans la bouteille cet *adjuventum* du talent qui les a fait atteindre à la crête escarpée de l'art."[101] Furthermore, a state of bold inspiration was indeed required in order to exploit fully the potentialities of the creative spirit: "Il faut donce être hors de soi, *amens*, pour être tout ce qu'on peut être."[102] And yet, he declined approval of Romantic indulgence in artificial stimulants to artistic productivity, preferring the example of Voltaire who required no such stimulation: "Heureux, qui, comme Voltaire et autres grands hommes, peut se trouver dans cet état inspiré, en buvant de l'eau et en se tenant au régime!"[103] His own abstemious and frugal habits during the working day (frequently omitting the midday meal in order to avoid the blunting

---

[99] *Ibid.* See Huyghe, *Delacroix*, p. 518 (n. 17) for a discussion of the relationship between Delacroix and Jenny.
[100] Medwin, *The Journal of the Conversations of Lord Byron*, pp. 195-96.
[101] *Journal*, I, p. 394 (July 21, 1850).
[102] *Ibid.*
[103] *Ibid.*

of artistic purpose) [104] demonstrate this austere principle in action. Fortunately his creative powers flowed freely without recourse to artificial stimulants. "Ma palette fraîchement arrangée et brillante du contraste des couleurs suffit pour allumer mon enthousiasme."[105] Yet, even had he been denied the gift of a naturally spontaneous fount of imagination, he would no doubt have declined the Hippocrene of gin and drugs. The overwhelming evidence of his commitment to the powers of reason explains his hostile attitude. This manner of attaining boldness would have provided only one aspect of the process of artistic creation while extinguishing the equally necessary control that only reason and judgment furnish.

In sum, Delacroix's thoughts on various aspects of the creative process reaffirm the dominant theme of his total aesthetic — the tempering of Romantic passion by the power of reason. He rejects fantastic flights of the imagination and retains a traditional definition of that faculty which favors a rational observance of reality. Although his predilection for sketchlike technique belongs to the progressive current of Romanticism, he cites traditional sources for its ability to attain spontaneity, brilliance, and stimulation of the imagination and acknowledges the benefits of finish in the final product. His rejection of Byron's bottle of gin in favor of Voltaire's glass of water is in keeping with this moderate position. His aim was to achieve creative ardor without abandoning the rational control that might be drowned in the artificially stimulating founts of Hippocrene.

[104] According to his friend, Léon Riesener, "son art a été le but de sa vie. Il lui a tout sacrifié et même en dernier lieu sa vie elle-même. Pour avoir la tête plus lucide, pour être plus propre au travail, il avait fini par supprimer le déjeuner et ne mangeait qu'une fois par jour." Information given to Philippe Burty by Riesener; see Philippe Burty, *Lettres de Eugène Delacroix*, p. xix. Already in 1668 Du Fresnoy had struck a similar puritanical note, claiming that "la peinture ne se plaît pas trop dans le vin ni dans la bonne chère . . ." Du Fresnoy, *L'Art de peinture*, p. 76.

[105] *Journal*, I, p. 392 (July 21, 1850).

CHAPTER IV

ASPECTS OF THE WORK

OF ART

BEAUTY

VICTOR HUGO enunciated one of the principal critical objections to Delacroix's art when he declared that, with few exceptions, notably the angelic figures in *Christ in the Garden of Gethsemane* of 1826 (Fig. 29) and the female nude of the *Massacre at Chios* of 1824 (Fig. 6), one searched in vain among his works for "une seule femme vraiment belle."[1] This alleged insensitivity to the beauty of the female form he considered symbolic of the artist's fundamental inability to create a representation of the beautiful: "Il a l'expression, mais il n'a pas l'idéal. Les *Femmes d'Alger,* par exemple, cette orientale étincelante de lumière et de couleur, sont le type de cette laideur exquise propre aux créations féminines de Delacroix."[2] Other critics of similar persuasion were C. P. Landon who claimed to discover in Delacroix's paintings a "système de laideur"[3] and Guyot de Fère who characterized his rendering of a scene from Chateaubriand, *The Natchez* of 1835 (Fig. 30), as a "peinture d'un aspect dégoûtant où la perspective aèrienne est si mal observée. . . . Quel étrange fanatisme de laideur tourmente cet artiste (je devrais dire ce peintre)!"[4] Against this background of

[1] From a conversation recorded by Charles Hugo in *Victor Hugo en Zélande*, Paris, 1868; quoted by Tourneux, *Eugène Delacroix devant ses contemporains*, p. 32.

[2] Tourneux, *op.cit.*, p. 32.

[3] C. P. Landon, "Scène des massacres de Scio," *Annales du musée*, Paris, 1824, p. 54; quoted by Horner, *Baudelaire: critique de Delacroix*, p. 15.

[4] Guyot de Fère, *Journal spécial des lettres et des beaux-arts*, Société d'encouragement pour les lettres et les beaux-arts, deuxième année, 1st vol., p. 204; quoted by Tourneux, *op.cit.*, p. 62.

hostile criticism it is no wonder that the nature of beauty became one of the major themes of the artist's written works — one that found expression in two articles, "Questions sur le beau," and "Des variations du beau."[5]

We have already noted that Delacroix was aware of Poussin's definition of beauty.[6] In the same entry of the Journal (January 1, 1857) he lists various theories of beauty that he found unsatisfactory — beauty as the good, the regular, the imitation of Raphael and the Antique — and turns instead to Voltaire for a more congenial definition, which stated that "nous n'appelons beau que ce qui cause à notre ame et à nos sens du plaisir et de l'admiration."[7] In view of his insistence on the crucial importance of the soul as the generating source of artistic content as well as the receptacle (in the spectator) of that content, his preference for Voltaire's definition is plausible. After all, in his article "Questions sur le beau," he too had endowed beauty with the ability to communicate with the soul claiming that "une belle action, un bel ouvrage, répondent à l'instant à une faculté de l'âme, sans doute à la plus noble."[8] This connection between beauty and the soul had already been anticipated by Addison who, in the *Spectator* paper of June 23, 1712, suggested that "there is nothing that makes its way more directly to the Soul than *Beauty*, which immediately diffuses a secret Satisfaction and Complacency through the Imagination, and gives a Finishing to anything that is Great or Uncommon."[9]

Less predictable than his stress on the importance of the relation between beauty and the soul is his attitude towards the humanist doctrine of beauty — doctrine that Rensselaer W. Lee has characterized as following "the common opinion of the ancients, on an harmonious proportion of parts, and is therefore, by contrast, a rational quality."[10] This doctrine, so popular during the Renaissance, was available to Delacroix, among many possibilities, in the

---

[5] "Questions sur le beau," appeared in *Revue des Deux-Mondes*, III, July 15, 1854, pp. 306-15; "Des variations du beau," appeared in the same publication, III, July 15, 1857, pp. 908-19. Both are reprinted in the first volume of Delacroix's *Œuvres littéraires*, the former on pp. 23-36 and the latter on pp. 37-54.
[6] See above p. 30 and n. 69.
[7] See above p. 30 and n. 71.   [8] *Œuvres littéraires*, I, p. 35.
[9] Addison and Steele, *The Spectator*, III, Vol. 6, p. 61; from paper no. 412.
[10] Rensselaer W. Lee, Review of *Artistic Theory in Italy: 1450-1600* by Anthony Blunt, *Art Bulletin*, XXIII (December 1941), p. 334.

work of Lodovico Dolce who affirmed that "la beauté ne provient que d'une proportion convenable, qui se trouve ordinairement dans le corps humain, et principalement à chaque membre en particulier."[11] The extraordinary vitality of this conception is apparent in its appearance, for one example, in the *Laocoon* of Lessing, who declared that "physical beauty results from the harmonious action of various parts which can be taken in at a glance."[12]

Delacroix, who, as a recognized leader of the Romantic Movement in painting, conceivably might have rejected a doctrine so patently nonorganic and inherently more congenial to Academic tastes, evidenced little hostility to this idea. Quite the contrary; in 1847 he defined beauty in this manner: "Le Beau est assurément la rencontre de toutes les convenances." The humanist tradition that colors this remark is evident in his characterization of the event that had inspired his thought; having witnessed a performance of Mozart's *Don Giovanni* the previous day, he praised it as an "admirable fusion de l'élégance, de l'expression, du bouffon, du terrible, du tendre, de l'ironique, chacun dans sa mesure."[13] In 1854, another evocation of Classical concepts of measure and proportion occurred when he declared that "le beau implique la réunion de plusieurs qualités: la force toute seule n'est pas la beauté sans la grâce, etc.: en un mot, l'harmonie en serait l'expression la plus large."[14] In both passages he retains Classical and Renaissance principles of measure and harmony while expanding the conception of these properties beyond the traditional formula. For, where Dolce, true to tradition, had interpreted measure and harmony as products of correct proportion of the visible parts, he, in a more searching way, proposed a balanced disposition not only of the elements of pictorial composition but also of nuances of expression. Hence his admiration for the harmonious fusion of elegance, comedy, horror, and irony embodied in Mozart's masterpiece.

This approval of a modified version of the humanist definition of beauty was not paralleled, however, by a correspondingly congenial reception of the Classical doctrine of ideal beauty. The

11 Dolce, *Dialogue sur la peinture, intitulé l'Aretin*, p. 119.
12 Lessing, *Laocoon*, p. 126.
13 *Journal*, I, pp. 186-87 (February 14, 1847).
14 *Journal*, II, p. 142 (1854).

theory of ideal beauty, especially as it had been expounded by Winckelmann, was still very much alive in the first half of the nineteenth century, notably in the writings of Quatremère de Quincy, who rejected simple reproduction of nature as the goal of art in favor of the realization of ideal types.[15] Delacroix, who was well aware of contemporary interest in this conception,[16] clearly opposed this position when, in 1851, he delivered an opinion that he felt would appear blasphemous in the eyes of most critics of his day. "Peut-être découvrira-t-on que Rembrandt," he suggested, "est un beaucoup plus grand peintre que Raphaël." Significantly, his evaluation rested on the realistic power of the Dutch artist as opposed to the ideal realm of the Italian artist who played such an influential role in Academic aesthetics: "J'écris ce blasphème propre à faire dresser les cheveux de tous les hommes d'école, sans prendre décidément parti; seulement je trouve en moi, à mesure que j'avance dans le vie, que la *vérité* est ce qu'il y a de plus beau et de plus rare."[17]

For this rejection of the Academic, Raphaelesque concept of ideal beauty in favor of Rembrandtesque truth as a more valid embodiment of the beautiful he discovered justification in literary sources. On August 25, 1859, for example, he excerpted from Boileau's *Preface* to the 1701 edition of his works a fervent appeal for truth — a truth basic to the achievement of beauty: "Puis donc qu'une pensée n'est belle qu'en ce qu'elle est vraie et que l'effet infaillible du vrai, quand il est bien énoncé, c'est de frapper les hommes, il s'ensuit que ce qui ne frappe point les hommes n'est ni beau ni vrai. . . ."[18] A similar equation of the true and the beautiful

---

[15] In art he desired "cet ensemble complet de beautés, de régularités, de perfections et d'harmonie, dont on demanderoit en vain à la nature une complète réunion dans aucun être vivant." Quatremère de Quincy, *Essai sur l'idéal dans ses applications pratiques*, Paris, 1837, p. 7. Also see René Schneider, *Quatremère de Quincy et son intervention dans les arts (1788-1830)*, Paris, 1910.

[16] On April 14, 1863, he noted in the Journal, the definition of beauty advanced by his friend Frédéric de Mercey, painter, author, and Chef de section des Beaux-Arts: "Je trouve dans mes calepins cette définition de Mercey, qui tranche l'équivoque entre la beauté qui ne consiste que dans les lignes pures, et celle qui consiste dans l'impression sur l'imagination par tout autre moyen: *Le Beau est le vrai idéalisé.*" *Journal*, III, p. 332.

[17] *Journal*, I, p. 439 (June 6, 1851).

[18] *Journal*, III, p. 228 (August 25, 1859). For the preface to the edition of

was available to him in another favorite source, the *Spectator,* where, in the paper of October 30, 1712, Addison had claimed that "no Thought is beautiful which is not just, and no Thought is just which is not founded in Truth, or at least in that which passes for such."[19] By truth, of course, Boileau and Addison both meant validity of general thought rather than adherence to surface reality. Yet the very fact of Delacroix's notation of Boileau's passage seems to reflect a desire to enjoy justification in traditional authority for his rejection of the Neo-Classical position.

In Addison one finds another concept that attracted Delacroix — the relativity of beauty. Symptomatic of the new tolerance for the various forms that appeared in the eighteenth century as opposed to the frequently narrow and dogmatic views of the previous century, Addison, in the *Spectator* paper of June 23, 1712, argued that "there is not perhaps any real Beauty or Deformity more in one piece of Matter than another, because we might have been so made, that whatsoever now appears loathsome to us, might have shewn itself agreeable. . . . Thus we see that every different Species of sensible Creatures has its different Notions of Beauty, and that each one of them is most affected with the Beauties of its own Kind."[20]

In 1855, Delacroix subscribed to the theory of the relativity of beauty, thereby suggesting the availability of the entire history of art production for study and emulation. "Le *beau*," he declared, "est partout, et . . . chaque homme non seulement le voit, mais doit absolument le rendre à sa manière."[21] His rejection of any narrow view of the occurrence of beauty is coupled, in this statement, with a corresponding liberty on the part of the artist to express beauty in any manner he deems fit.

In keeping with this liberal attitude he also embraced the notion of the subjectivity of the beautiful proclaiming that "chaque homme de talent a, en lui, des types particuliers de vrai et de beau."[22] The element of subjectivity in the appreciation of the

1701, see *Œuvres complètes de Boileau Despréaux*, pp. 179-81. The excerpt quoted (with a few minor discrepancies) by Delacroix occurs on p. 180.

[19] Addison and Steele, *The Spectator*, IV, Vol. 7, p. 182; from paper no. 523.

[20] *Ibid.*, III, Vol. 6, p. 61; from paper no. 412.

[21] *Journal*, II, p. 395 (October 1, 1855).

[22] From his notes for the article, "Questions sur le beau." See *Œuvres littéraires*, I, p. 143.

beautiful had previously been connected, in the Horatian manner, with the taste of the individual. De Piles, for example, stated: "Le Beau . . . n'est rien de réel, chacun en juge selon son goût; en un mot, que le Beau n'est autre chose que ce qui plaît."[23] For Delacroix, of course, the expression of the beautiful as dependent upon sources within the individual artist goes far beyond de Piles' paraphrase of the Horatian formula. His conception is a mature Romantic one which derives, no doubt, from the writings of Madame de Staël who, in her explication of Kant's *Critique of Judgment*, expounded the Kantian idea: "De cette explication du sentiment de l'infini aux beaux-arts [by Kant] doit naître l'idéal, c'est-à-dire le beau, considéré non pas comme la réunion et l'imitation de ce qu'il y a de mieux dans la nature, mais comme l'image réalisée de ce que notre âme se représente."[24]

Another Romantic conception of beauty conditioned his thought and, demonstrably, his art. From Senancour's *Obermann* of 1804, he cited, in 1857,[25] a passage of striking significance for one of the notable characteristics of his own art: "Le joli amuse la pensée, le beau soutient l'âme, le sublime l'étonne ou l'exalte; mais ce qui séduit et passionne les cœurs, ce sont des beautés plus vagues et plus étendues encore, peu connues, jamais expliquées, mystérieuses et ineffables."[26]

Exploitation of vagueness and obscurity as vehicles of Romantic suggestion frequently appears in Romantic art. For Delacroix, however, Senancour's statement has particular significance since it provided justification for these elements not only for their expressive function but also their enhancement of beauty — a beauty no longer characterized by the bright, clear, unproblematical images of the Neo-Classicists.

Although the notation of Senancour's dictum appears in the Journal in 1857, Delacroix's art throughout its development frequently exploited this Romantic device. The *Dante and Virgil* of 1822 (Fig. 5) already depends upon a vague, smoldering background (the burning city of Dis) for much of its effect; the deep

[23] De Piles, *Cours de peinture par principes*, p. 135.
[24] Madame de Staël, *De l'Allemagne*, p. 454.
[25] *Journal*, III, p. 84 (March 22, 1857).
[26] For the source of this quotation, see Étienne Pivert de Senancour, *Oberman: Lettres publiées par M. . . . Senancour*, Grenoble, 1947, I, p. 95; from letter 21.

recess of the hall in *Boissy d'Anglas at the Convention* of 1831 (Fig. 25) evokes a heavy and ominous setting for the violent activity of the protagonists; the indeterminate and mysterious milieu in which St. George confronts the dragon (1847; Fig. 26) suggests a palpable atmosphere of danger and evil; and in the late version of *Medea* (1862; Fig. 31) the noble and distraught heroine contemplates her terrible revenge in a vague, cavernous setting in which the dark, rocky masses seem to dissolve into menacing, somehow weightless stormclouds that sympathetically respond to the storm raging in her soul. In all these examples Delacroix derives maximum expressive power from this technique; yet, he must also have intended, in the Obermannian sense, a quality of beauty, albeit a wild, Romantic beauty alien to Neo-Classical theory and practice.

Indulgence in the vague and formless carried with it further fuel for those critics who saw in his work the disintegration of Neo-Classical standards, thereby stimulating his interest in another traditional topic — the correct relationship between unity and variety.

UNITY AND VARIETY

Delécluze, always the most hostile of critics, found in the *Death of Sardanapalus* (Fig. 6) a lack of rational structure which prevented any appeal to the prescribed destination of Neo-Classical endeavor — the mind. "L'intelligence du spectateur," he wrote, "n'a pu pénétrer dans un sujet dont tous les détails sont isolés, où l'œil ne peut débrouiller la confusion des lignes et des couleurs, où les premières règles de l'art semblent avoir été violées de partis pris. Le *Sardanapale* est une erreur du peintre."[27] Delacroix, however, was acutely aware of this problem. We have already noted that he considered unfortunate Rubens' occasional lapses into "un affreux désordre."[28] And in Michelangelo's art he detected certain reprehensible elements of disorganization. The *Last Judgment* of the Sistine Chapel, in particular, violated a traditional rule that he deemed of fundamental importance — the subordination of detail. "Je n'y vois que des détails frappants, frappants comme un coup de poing qu'on reçoit; mais l'intérêt, l'unité, l'enchaînement de tout cela est absent."[29] Indeed,

---

[27] Quoted by Tourneux, *Eugène Delacroix devant ses contemporains*, p. 49.
[28] *Journal*, I, p. 168 (January 25, 1847).
[29] *Journal*, II, p. 282 (October 4, 1854).

abuse of detail with its subsequent loss of unity became one of his critical touchstones — one that he applied as well to works of literature.[30] Convinced of the validity of this criterion, he declared that "le grand artiste concentre l'intérêt en supprimant les détails inutiles ou repoussants ou sots...."[31]

This insistence on the subordination of detail relies upon a long-standing tradition that flourished during the Renaissance, assumed primary status in the seventeenth century among the tenets of the French Academy, and lingered as an important concept in the writings of eighteenth-century theorists. In the fifteenth century, Alberti, with reference to pictorial composition, described the dangers of overabundant variety in painting: "I blame those painters who, where they wish to appear copious, leave nothing vacant. It is not composition but dissolute confusion which they disseminate."[32] In the next century, Lodovico Dolce, in more general terms, utters a note of caution: "Parlons à présent de la variété laquelle doit être pratiquée par le peintre, comme une partie si essentielle, que sans elle la beauté, et l'art deviennent à charge .... Mais sur ce point il faut aussi prendre garde de ne pas donner dans l'excés...."[33] In France this doctrine appears in the theory of Poussin who, according to Bellori, declared that the "first care [of the painter] should be to avoid minute details as much as he possibly can, in order not to violate the fitness of the theme...."[34] In the realm of literary theory, Boileau stated, in *L'Art poétique*, the same requirement: "Fuyez de ces auteurs l'abondance stérile,/ Et ne vous chargez point d'un détail inutile."[35]

The subordination of detail to the dictates of the larger design of the grand style was still espoused in the eighteenth century by Sir Joshua Reynolds, who declared that "the whole beauty and grandeur of the art consists, in my opinion, in being able to get above all

---

[30] Of contemporary literature in the naturalistic mode he wrote: "Ce qui fait l'infériorité de la littérature moderne, c'est la prétention de tout rendre; l'ensemble disparaît noyé dans les détails et l'ennui en est la conséquence." *Œuvres littéraires*, I, p. 62.

[31] *Journal*, II, p. 174 (April 28, 1854).

[32] Alberti, *On Painting*, pp. 75-76.

[33] Dolce, *Dialogue sur la peinture, intitulé l'Aretin*, p. 203.

[34] Nicolas Poussin, "Observations on Painting," in Holt, *Literary Sources of Art History*, p. 368.

[35] *Œuvres complètes de Boileau Despréaux*, p. 242.

singular forms, local customs, particularities, and details of every kind."[36] One should also note that other motivations for this principle appeared at this time. Voltaire, in *Discours sur la tragédie*, which Delacroix knew, stated a law of diminishing emotive returns deriving from the overlavish use of grisly details in battle scenes: "Plus une action théâtrale est majestueuse ou effrayante, plus elle deviendrait insipide, si elle était souvent répétée; à-peu-pres comme les détails des batailles, qui, étant par eux-mêmes ce qu'il y a de plus terribles, deviennent froids et ennuyeux, à force de reparaître souvent dans les histoires."[37]

Diderot gives us (in his *Essai sur la peinture*) the closest anticipation of Delacroix's interpretation of this matter. Though granting the need for variety, he regretted the tendency of profuse detail to dilute the force of the whole: "Ce n'est pas assez que d'avoir bien établi l'ensemble, il s'agit d'y introduire les détails, sans détruire la masse."[38] While sketching a preliminary idea for the *Entombment* of 1848 (Fig. 32), Delacroix articulated his awareness of this problem in words that are reminiscent of Diderot's: "Je suis satisfait de cette ébauche, mais comment conserver, en ajoutant des détails, cette impression d'ensemble qui résulte de masses très simples?"[39]

In general, Delacroix's art, over the years, shows an increasing ability to heed the advice of these writers in curbing his youthful indulgence in extravagant detail. In two of his very early key works — *Massacre at Chios* of 1824 (Fig. 7) and *Death of Sardanapalus* of 1827 (Fig. 6) — one observes clearly a lack of compositional and psychological unity heightened by an almost orgiastic display of color, pattern, and texture. In the earlier picture he renders the accoutrement of the Turkish rider with a brilliant, rich pigment that succeeds in awakening the eye to their visually exciting qualities. In similar fashion, the radiant and subtly harmonious color patterns of the dress of the seated old woman detract from the essential tragic content of the picture. Indeed, these seductive parts, in conjunction with the disruptive composition, force the spectator

[36] *Sir Joshua Reynolds: Discourses on Art*, p. 44; from the Third Discourse of December 14, 1770.
[37] Voltaire, *Œuvres complètes*, III, p. 383.
[38] Diderot, *Essais sur la peinture*, p. 41.
[39] *Journal*, I, p. 196 (March 1, 1847).

to experience the work piecemeal rather than as a whole. And, in the general disarray of the *Sardanapalus*, an overly abundant profusion of accessories — arms, vases, jewelry — clutter the foreground.

It is only fair to point out, however, that the existence of these distracting details fails to destroy the undeniable power both pictures generate. One might even argue that the very riot of colorful detail contributes to the tumultuous emotional effect of the scenes. Furthermore, Delacroix might well have excused himself by an appeal to the traditional prerogatives of genius which allowed, in the illustrious examples of Shakespeare, Homer, Pindar, and Corneille, occasional lapses from serene and consistent perfection. Still, in total unity of effect, the pictures do err. And, in his mature period, when the attractions of formless, Romantic expression had given way to an interest in a more unified manner of expressing Romantic content, the subordination of detail became a cardinal element of his style. The *Entombment*, for which he had sought, in preliminary work, to discover the proper relationship between detail and mass, demonstrates the unity achieved by the adoption of this traditional principle. No longer do individual parts offer seductive traps for the eye. All details irrelevant to the expression of spiritual and emotive content recede and merge in the generalized atmosphere of tragic calm. As a generalized statement neither Poussin nor Reynolds would have found in it grounds for censure. It represents, in a sense, the Grand Style reborn, but the Grand Style harnessed now for the purpose of Romantic expression. It conforms, as well, to the criterion established by Baudelaire when he wrote, in his Salon of 1846: "l'art, n'étant qu'une abstraction et un sacrifice du détail à l'ensemble, il est important de s'occuper surtout des masses."[40]

A preoccupation with the role of detail constitutes but one aspect of Delacroix's conception of unity in painting. It is interesting to note that despite his indebtedness in so many issues to Madame de Staël's formulation of German Romantic aesthetics he did not

[40] From Baudelaire's Salon of 1846; see *Curiosités esthétiques* . . . , p. 107. For the influence of Delacroix's theory on Baudelaire, see especially Margaret Gilman, *Baudelaire the Critic*, esp. pp. 9-40; Lucie Horner, *Baudelaire: critique de Delacroix*, esp. pp. 1-10; René Jullian, "Delacroix et Baudelaire," *Gazette des Beaux-Arts*, Dec. 1953, pp. 311-26; and René Huyghe, "Delacroix et Baudelaire," *The Arts Yearbook*, ii, 1958, pp. 27-46.

espouse the theory of organic form.[41] An inherent predilection for unity no doubt prevented his adoption of an idea that allowed the artist complete freedom in his formal embodiment of expressive content. Even the spectator, in his view, possessed an innate need for formal order in his experience of a work of art: "Un tableau qui semble devoir satisfaire plus complètement et plus facilement ce besoin d'unité, puisqu'il semble qu'on le voie tout d'une fois, ne le produit pas davantage s'il n'est bien composé. . . ."[42]

Moreover, it was this essential quality of unity that served as a criterion when he judged artists of the past. He considered Poussin, whom he fundamentally admired, remiss in this respect. "Il semble que toutes ses figures sont sans lien les unes avec les autres et semblent découpées; de là ces lacunes et cette absence d'unité, de fondu, d'effet, qui se trouvent dans Lesueur et dans tous les coloristes."[43] Rembrandt, on the other hand, provided him a sterling example of painterly unity — far surpassing even Rubens in whose *Lot Fleeing from Sodom* of 1625[44] he criticized the "froideur de cette composition et du peu d'intérêt qu'elle présente. . . ." It was Rembrandt who had discovered true pictorial unity by means of adjustment of accessories and the principal subject: "Véritablement ce n'est qu'à Rembrandt qu'on voit commencer, dans les tableaux, cet accord des accessoires et du sujet principal, qui me paraît à moi

[41] For the German formulation of the doctrine of organic form, see especially August Wilhelm Schlegel, *Lectures on Dramatic Art and Literature*, tr. J. Black, London, 1894, p. 340, wherein he states: "Form is mechanical when, through external force, it is imparted to any material merely as an accidental addition without reference to its quality; as, for example, when we give a particular shape to a soft mass that it may retain the same after its induration. Organical form, again, is innate, it unfolds itself from within, and acquires its determination contemporaneously with the perfect development of the germ." The best treatment of organic form and its role in Romantic aesthetics is in M. H. Abrams, *The Mirror and the Lamp*, pp. 198-225. Also helpful are Stephen C. Pepper, *World Hypotheses*, Berkeley and Los Angeles, 1942, pp. 280-314, and Donald D. Egbert, "Organic Expression and Architecture," *Evolutionary Thought in America*, ed. S. Persons, New Haven, 1950, pp. 336-96.

[42] *Journal*, ii, pp. 155-56 (March 26, 1854).

[43] *Journal*, i, p. 439 (June 6, 1851). This preference for Lesueur rests, of course, on his own predilection for color as an expressive device. Traditional concepts of color as a unifying element will be discussed later in this chapter.

[44] In 1862 (according to the catalogue of the centennial exhibition in Bordeaux, *Delacroix: ses maîtres, ses amis, ses élèves*, Bordeaux, 1963, no. 58, pl. 4), Delacroix painted a copy of Rubens' work in which certain changes — suppression of detail, more closely knit grouping of the figures, and simplification of the architectural setting — alleviate some of the compositional faults he discerned in the model.

une des parties les plus importantes, si ce n'est pas la plus importante."[45] Unlike Poussin, Rembrandt harmonized figures and background: "Chez Rembrandt même — et ceci est la perfection — le
fond et les figures ne font qu'un. L'intérêt est partout: vous ne
divisez rien, comme dans une belle vue que vous offre la nature et
où tout concourt à vous enchanter."[46]

Having extolled Rembrandt for his achievement of the close-
knit unity that he found essential in any work of art, Delacroix
elsewhere attacked the traditional French conception of unity,
which in turn depended on the art theory of the Italian Renaissance.
As late as 1860, when, according to certain writers, he had assumed
in his theory a rigidly classical pose, he assailed the Academic conception of pictorial unity. French Academic theory, he argued, had,
on the basis of Classical example, confined art to a straitjacket of
codified, sterile principles of unity. In a penetrating strain of
irony (evident when the passage is considered in context) he evokes
the conventional means of unifying a composition: "Il faut que
toutes les parties, ingénieuses ou non, concourent dans une certaine
mesure à la connexion du tout. . . ."[47] The coherent relationship of
the parts to one another as well as to the whole had constituted one
of the basic principles of Renaissance unity, appearing early in the
writings of Alberti and adopted later by Leonardo and Dürer.[48]
Delacroix, however, held that French art, especially when compared
with the more natural and irregular expression of Shakespeare, had
become sterile in its automatic repetition of devices designed to
achieve regularity and symmetry. "Le système français," he proposed,
"est evidemment le résultat de combinaisons très ingénieuses, pour
donner à l'impression plus de nerf, plus d'unité, c'est-à-dire quelque
chose de plus artiste; mais il en résulte que chez les plus grands
maîtres, ces moyens sont petits et puérils et nuisent, à leur manière,

[45] *Journal*, II, p. 212 (July 5, 1854). Delacroix adds to this remark further
evidence of interest in Roger de Piles' *Balance des peintres*: "On pourrait
faire à ce sujet [adjustment of accessories and main subject] une comparaison
entre les maîtres fameux."

[46] *Journal*, II, p. 219 (July 29, 1854).

[47] *Journal*, III, p. 273 (March 3, 1860).

[48] See the discussion of their conceptions by K. E. Gilbert and H. Kuhn, *A
History of Esthetics*, New York, 1939, pp. 186-90. According to the authors (p.
187), harmony for Alberti, Leonardo, and Dürer meant "complete agreement
of the different parts of the art object with each other and with the whole."

à l'impression, par le nécessité de ressorts artificiels, de préparations, etc. . . . . Ainsi ce système amène la régularité et une sorte de froide symétrie plutôt que l'unité."[49]

Although these hostile statements confirm his rejection of the traditional concept of unity — a system which prevented the achievement of pictorial unity in the Rembrandtian sense, his own conception did not incorporate the freedom allowed by the advocates of organic unity. It did rely, however, on a mixture of preromantic and romantic ideas. The concept of unity as a necessary ingredient of beauty derived from two specific sources — Diderot's *Pensées détachées* and Senancour's *Obermann*. Diderot had linked unity with beauty claiming that "rien n'est beau sans unité."[50] And Senancour, in his influential work of 1804, echoed this statement in words which Delacroix copied in the Journal in 1857: "Ce tout est *l'unité* sans laquelle il n'y a pas de résultat, ni d'ouvrage qui puisse être beau, parce qu'alors il n'y a pas même d'ouvrage."[51]

Sharing this homage to beauty and unity, Delacroix, as a practicing artist, also sought concrete means of achieving these qualities. In addition to the subordination of detail, he exploited a visual equivalent for unity that was to foreshadow Impressionistic devices.[52] In the Journal entry of January 25, 1857, one discovers a paragraph devoted to a topic entitled *Liaison* which may best be translated (following Walter Pach) as "binding together." Here he poses a conception of unity achieved by means of atmospheric cohesion — an idea rooted in traditional theory which he was destined to carry much farther.

Writers on art had long been concerned with the value of atmospheric effects. Leonardo, in his notebooks, had analyzed with extraordinary prophetic power the minute variations of reflected lights.[53] His attention was centered, however, on the objectively observed nature of this phenomenon. The unifying attributes of atmosphere are described later, appearing in the *Cours de peinture*

[49] *Journal*, III, pp. 440-41 (*Supplément*).

[50] Diderot, *Essais sur la peinture*, p. 129.

[51] The italics are Delacroix's. For the source of Delacroix's quotation, see Senancour, *Oberman: Lettres publiées par M. . . . Senancour*, I, p. 92; from letter 21. The quotation appears in the *Journal*, III, p. 83.

[52] See in this connection Paul Signac, *D'Eugène Delacroix au néo-impressionisme*, Paris, 1939 (1st ed., 1899), and Lee Johnson, *Delacroix*, London, 1963.

[53] See especially Leonardo da Vinci, *Treatise on Painting*, I, pp. 76-81.

par principes of de Piles, who conceived of a *Tout-ensemble* that comprised "une liaison de plusieurs objets . . . point comme un nombre composé de plusieurs unitez indépendantes et égales entre elles. . . . Tous les objets qui entrent dans le Tableau, toutes les lignes et toutes les couleurs, toutes les lumières et toutes les ombres ne sont grandes ou petites, fortes ou foibles que par comparaison."[54] For Delacroix atmospheric effects become one of the chief means of achieving harmony and unity, with reflections playing a major role. "Quand nous jetons les yeux sur les objets qui nous entourent, que ce soit un paysage ou un intérieur, nous remarquons entre les objets qui s'offrent à nos regards une sorte de liaison produite par l'atmosphère qui les enveloppe et par les reflets de toutes sortes qui font en quelque sorte participer chaque objet à une sorte d'harmonie générale."[55]

The progressive aspect of this concept lies in its clear anticipation of Impressionist and Neo-Impressionist techniques.[56] Less evident, perhaps, is the probable source of Delacroix's idea. For already in the previous century Diderot had conceived of the function of light and reflection in terms so similar that it is tempting to interpret Delacroix's statement as a paraphrase of Diderot. In reference to still-life painting Diderot advised: "Assemblez confusément des objets de toute espèce et de toutes couleurs, du linge, des fruits, du papier, des livres, des étoffes, et des animaux, et vous verrez que l'air et la lumière, ces deux harmoniques universels, les accorderont tous, je ne sais comment, par des reflets imperceptibles, tout se liera, les disparates s'affaibliront, et votre œil ne reprochera rien à l'ensemble."[57]

While Diderot can be credited with the theoretical formulation of this proto-Impressionist conception, it was Delacroix who in practice anticipated the manipulation of effects of light and atmosphere that would appear in the works of Monet, Renoir, and others. Consider *Sea at Dieppe* of 1852 (Fig. 33) which already contains hints of Impressionist technique especially in its use of loose, autonomous brushstrokes to render the hazy, luminous effect of

[54] De Piles, *Cours de peinture par principes*, pp. 104-5.

[55] *Journal*, III, p. 41 (January 25, 1857).

[56] For a discussion of Delacroix's important role in this development, see Signac, *op.cit.*, esp. pp. 18-22.

[57] From the Salon of 1763; see *Œuvres complètes de Diderot*, X, p. 187.

sunset light filtering through heavy clouds and broken strokes to emphasize the reflections of solid objects in water. Monet would merely state these items more decisively in a work such as his *Impression: Rising Sun* of 1872 (Fig. 34) where the unifying possibilities of light, atmosphere, and reflections successfully suggested by Delacroix are fully exploited with the resultant disappearance of traditional depth and the emergence of a new textural unity at the level of the picture surface.

With all these progressive insights into future Impressionist approaches Delacroix, however, still utilized these advanced technical procedures not only for the attainment of greater pictorial unity but also for the expression of Romantic content. In comparison with Monet's emotionally discreet manipulation of pictorial devices *Sea at Dieppe* assumes a more enigmatic aspect. The effect of the sunset light burnishing the clouds with a hectic glow, the broad, dark accents of the brushstrokes which depict the rippling water in the foreground, and the ominous jutting prow of the boat — all tend to evoke an image of natural beauty suffused, especially in the foreground, with some forbidding and melancholy meaning. Fortunately, in the Journal, Delacroix has recorded his psychological frame of mind before such a seascape. On Tuesday, September 14, 1852, he had suffered particularly from his chronic throat condition: "Ma dernière journée à Dieppe n'a pas été la meilleure. J'avais la gorge irritée d'avoir trop parlé la veille." The physical irritation caused by the flaring up of the ailment that was eventually to cause his death induced in him feelings of nostalgia and regret at the thought of leaving the entrancing seascape before him: "J'ai été faire ma dernière visite à la mer, vers trois heures. Elle était du plus beau calme et une des plus belles que j'aie vues. Je ne pouvais m'en arracher. . . . L'âme s'attache avec passion aux objets que l'on va quitter."[58] The melancholy and pessimism inherent in this statement find visual expression in the dark and ominous elements that cast a baleful influence on the seductive beauty of the scene. In conjunction with the warning resurgence of his throat condition his soul feels an intense desire to fix on the surrounding beauty which under the circumstances takes on a melancholy, be-

[58] *Journal*, I, p. 487 (September 14, 1852).

cause ephemeral, aspect. No wonder, then, that the dark, fore-boding waves and the prow of the boat assume a supra-pictorial purpose. They suggest gloom and despair in the face of impending fate much as the crows winging towards the spectator in Van Gogh's *Crows Over the Wheat Field* (Fig. 35) serve as harbingers of on-rushing doom.

Clearly, then, Delacroix, unlike many Romantic artists of the nineteenth century, was reluctant to abandon traditional form as a basic ingredient in art. Compelled by an innate sense of unity, he detected formlessness even in the works of Rubens and Michel-angelo. In the works of more contemporary artists — Romantic musicians such as Beethoven and Realist writers such as Balzac — he noted a tendency towards lack of unity that marred the clarity of their expressive designs. In order to combat their frequent lapse into superfluous detail, he relied upon the concept of subordination of detail which had been one of the keystones of humanist art theory and which had further support in the writings of Diderot. And in his mature works he consciously strove to restrain the exuberant proliferation of detail evident in the works of his youth.

While he never espoused the Romantic principle of organic unity, he nevertheless endeavored with conspicuous success to abandon the traditional principle of unity based on the concept of formal inter-relationship and to create a new pictorial unity that would rival, though achieved by different means, the painterly unity of Rem-brandt. Aware of Senancour's suggestion that unity was necessary for the attainment of beauty, he forged a new technique for pictorial unity based on the depiction of light, atmosphere, and reflection through the use of broken and throbbing brushstrokes that anticipates the procedures of Impressionist painting. Yet, even in this progressive role, his achievement is based on antecedent theory — ostensibly, in this case, on the example of Diderot.

REGULARITY

Related to the problem of the adjustment of unity and variety is the problem of the proper degree of regularity required in a work of art. In the bracing air of freedom of expressive means accorded Romantic artists, the temptation to reject this notion entirely out of hand must have been great. Delacroix pondered much on the matter and advocated, in the main, a loosening of the bonds of regularity. As always, however, his position is not a simple one. He must have been extremely sensitive to the hostile remarks of critics who claimed that he painted "sans égard aux proportions, au dessin, aux plus habituelles conventions de l'art"[59] or in a manner harmful to "l'unité du plan et la régularité des formes."[60] At any rate, he adopted a duality of approach which, while favoring the abandonment of regularity when necessary, nevertheless appreciated the advantages conferred by this principle.

In the traditional manner he often equated regularity with Classicism, speaking at one point in the Journal of "ces types grecs, cette régularité dont on s'est habitué à faire le type invariable du beau."[61] And on another occasion, on January 13, 1857 (while defining the nature of Classical art for the preliminary sketch of the Dictionnaire), he dogmatically declared regularity to be one of the essential features of Antique works of art: "J'appellerais volontiers classiques tous les ouvrages réguliers, ceux qui satisfont l'esprit non seulement par une peinture exacte ou grandiose ou piquante des sentiments et des choses, mais encore par l'unité, l'ordonnance logique, en un mot par toutes ces qualités qui augmentent l'impression en amenant la simplicité."[62]

Despite this sincere admiration of Classical art and the frequent manifestation of certain Classical principles in his own art, he was overtly suspicious of those who would attribute the successful expression achieved in any work of art to the quality of regularity. Even in the works of Mozart, whom he regarded as a serene and consistent genius, he discovered a vital substratum that belied any appearance of surface regularity, deploring the attitude of those persons who denied the existence of "cette partie vitale, cette force secrète, qui est tout Shakespeare. . . . Il leur faut absolument l'alexandrin et le contrepoint: ils n'admirent, dans Mozart, que la régularité."[63]

---

[59] By the critic, Chauvin, in his Salon of 1824; quoted by Tourneux, *Eugène Delacroix devant ses contemporains*, p. 44.

[60] By a critic identified as "D," reviewing the Salon of 1824 in the *Moniteur universel*, September 8, 1824; quoted by Tourneux, *op.cit.*, p. 44.

[61] *Journal*, II, p. 395 (October 1, 1855).

[62] *Journal*, III, p. 23 (January 13, 1857).

[63] *Journal*, II, p. 357 (July 16, 1855).

The status of regularity as a primary element in art had not gone unquestioned in the history of aesthetics. Already in the third century, Plotinus had suggested that "since the one face, constant in symmetry, appears sometimes fair and sometimes not, can we doubt that beauty is something more than symmetry."[64] And even during the height of French aspiration toward Classical form in the seventeenth century, there appeared several warnings against the rigid application of the principle of regularity. La Fontaine discovered that "le secret de plaire ne consiste pas toujours en l'ajustement ni même en la régularité; il faut du piquant et de l'agréable si l'on veut toucher."[65] La Rochefoucauld, while admitting the frequent importance of regularity for the achievement of true beauty, described another type of beauty, often evident in women who possessed a kind of "beauté éclatante, mais irrégulière."[66] In the eighteenth century, of course, all reservations concerning the necessity of irregularity tended to disappear so that Diderot could banish one form of regularity — symmetry — from its former position. In his *Pensées détachées* he defined symmetry as "l'égalité des parties correspondantes dans un tout," and dogmatically states that "la symétrie, essentielle dans l'architecture, est bannie de tout genre de peinture."[67]

On October 1, 1855, Delacroix, in the course of a discussion of regularity, posed the problem in terms of the beauty of the female countenance, recalling the example of Plotinus and La Rochefoucauld: "Les femmes ne plaisent pas seulement par la régularité des traits; il en est qui sont pourvues de cet avantage et qui ne nous disent rien."[68] Eight months later, on May 30, 1856, he cited confirmation for this traditional idea which he found in the writings of Edgar Allan Poe. From Baudelaire's translation of Poe's fantastic tale, *Ligeia*, he copied a passage which accords irregularity of features the power to evoke female beauty. The quotation appears in the Journal in this manner:

Quant à la beauté de la figure, aucune femme ne l'a jamais

[64] Plotinus, *The Ethical Treatises*, tr. S. Mackenna, London, 1917, I, pp. 78-79.
[65] Jean de la Fontaine, *Œuvres*, ed. H. Regnier, Paris, 1883-97, IV, p. 147.
[66] François de la Rochefoucauld, "Réflexions diverses," *Œuvres de la Rochefoucauld*, ed. M. D. L. Gilbert, Paris, 1868, I, p. 72.
[67] Diderot, *Essais sur la peinture*, p. 129.
[68] *Journal*, II, p. 396.

égalée . . . Cependant ses traits n'étaient pas jetés dans ce moule régulier qu'on nous a faussement enseigné à révérer dans les ouvrages classiques du paganisme: *Il n'y a pas de beauté exquise, dit lord Verulam [Francis Bacon], parlant avec justesse de tous les genres de beauté, sans une certaine étrangeté dans les proportions.* (Edgar Poë, *Ligéra*).[69]

Since this passage mentions Francis Bacon as an earlier advocate of this idea, it embodies the principle that frequently underlay Delacroix's search for congenial formulas in the realm of art theory — a double authority, coupling a time-hallowed source with a more contemporary example, thus satisfying that aspect of his tempered Romanticism which required traditional support for an anti-Classical notion.

Further authority for this idea was available to Delacroix in the *Discourses* of Reynolds, who paraphrased Bacon's words on the subject ("There is no excellent beauty that hath not some strangeness in the proportion"[70]) and cited his amplification of this conception, which later found its way into Poe's work. In Bacon's words: "A man cannot tell whether Apelles or Albert Dürer were the more trifler; whereof the one would make a personage by geometrical proportions, the other, by taking the best parts out of divers faces, to make one excellent."[71]

As in so many other cases, however, Delacroix's position on the problem of regularity is equivocal. Notwithstanding his predominant approval of the progressive factor of irregularity, which allowed the Romantic artist liberation from exterior restraints, he took cautious note of the advantages conferred by adherence to regularity. For he recognized the limits beyond which the irregularity of a work of art might begin to function as a detrimental factor. Significantly, he took a Romantic musician to task for violation of this principle. "Dans les arts, tels que la littérature ou la musique," he insisted, "il est essentiel d'établir une grande proportion dans les

---

[69] *Journal*, II, p. 450 (May 30, 1856). For the source of the quotation, see Edgar Poe, *Histoires extraordinaires*, tr. Charles Baudelaire, Paris, 1875, pp. 297-98.

[70] Francis Bacon, "Of Beauty," *Bacon's Essays*, ed. R. Whately, London, 1856, p. 395.

[71] *Ibid.*, pp. 395-96. Reynolds' quotation of the passage (in somewhat abbreviated form) occurs in the Third Discourse of December 14, 1770; see *Sir Joshua Reynolds: Discourses on Art*, p. 46.

parties qui composent l'ouvrage. Les morceaux de Beethoven trop longs. Il fatigue en occupant trop longtemps de la même idée."[72]

If this violation of regularity of proportion in music seemed reprehensible, consider how fatal it was in the more tangible art of architecture. In a virulent attack on Gothic Revival architecture in France (an unusual attitude for a Romantic artist), Delacroix evoked the regularly proportioned forms of the Renaissance as a desirable antidote to contemporary lapses: "Après les ténèbres du moyen age, la Renaissance, qui a été véritablement celle du goût, c'est-à-dire du bon sens, c'est-à-dire du beau dans tous les genres; on est revenu à ces proportions admirables dont il faudra toujours, en dépit de toutes les prétentions à l'originalité, reconnaître l'empire incontestable."[73]

This mordant view of the Gothic as "des siècles de barbarie" accords well with dominant seventeenth- and eighteenth-century attitudes[74] and recalls the words of Montesquieu, who in the *Essai sur le goût* described the Gothic style in disparaging terms: "Un bâtiment d'ordre gothique est une espèce d'énigme pour l'œil qui le voit; et l'âme est embarrassée comme quand on lui présente un poëme obscur."[75] Like Delacroix, he turned to Classical symmetry as the proper corrective, claiming that "une des principales causes des plaisirs de notre âme lorsqu'elle voit des objets, c'est la facilité qu'elle a à les apercevoir; et la raison qui fait que la symétrie plaît à l'âme, c'est qu'elle lui épargne de la peine, qu'elle la soulage, et qu'elle coupe, pour ainsi dire, l'ouvrage par la moitié."[76]

In short, though favoring the Romantic principle of irregularity as advocated by both contemporary and traditional authority, Dela-

---

[72] *Journal*, III, p. 16 (January 13, 1857).

[73] *Ibid.*, p. 255 (January 27, 1860).

[74] For seventeenth- and eighteenth-century attitudes towards the Gothic, see especially Kenneth Clark, *The Gothic Revival*, London, 1928; Arthur O. Lovejoy, "The First Gothic Revival and the Return to Nature," *Modern Language Notes*, XXVII (1932), pp. 414-46; Agnes Addison, *Romanticism and the Gothic Revival*, New York, 1938, esp. pp. 22-55; and Paul Frankl, *The Gothic: Literary Sources and Interpretations through Eight Centuries*, Princeton, 1960, pp. 329-414.

[75] Charles Louis Secondat de Montesquieu, "Essai sur le goût dans les choses de la nature et de l'art," *Œuvres complètes*, V, p. 173.

[76] *Ibid.*, p. 174.

croix retained an option on regularity as a means of curbing possible excesses of Romantic expression.

COLOR

During the first half of the nineteenth century, artistic circles in France witnessed a revival of the controversy concerning the primacy of color or line which had flourished during the last quarter of the seventeenth century. At this time the advocates of line had exalted Poussin as their champion while the colorists rallied around the example of Rubens.[77] Repeating the situation of the earlier period, a Neo-Classical faction championed the intellectual and austere qualities of line while the more progressive group (chiefly artists of the Romantic persuasion) exploited the sensuous and emotive possibilities of color.

Delacroix's role as a propagandist for color is well known. This commitment was due, at least in part, to his aversion to the styles of David and Ingres where line dominated color. Delécluze, in his biography of David, cites with relish that master's advice to a student who had demonstrated a reprehensible taste of coloristic devices. To the unlucky novice, David exclaimed: "Tu fais passer le dessin après la couleur. Eh bien, mon cher ami, c'est mettre la charrue avant les boeufs."[78] Later, Ingres displayed a similar predilection for contour. "La couleur," he conceded, "ajoute des ornements à la peinture; mais elle n'en est que la dame d'atours, puisqu'elle ne fait que rendre plus aimables les véritables perfections de l'art."[79]

Needless to say, Delacroix, despite a generous admiration for some aspects of Ingres' art, firmly rejected his conception of color both in theory and in practice. During a lively conversation on the subject with George Sand (recorded in her *Impressions et souvenirs*), he derided Ingres' practice: "Il [Ingres] confond la coloration avec la couleur . . . Avez-vous remarqué que, dans la *Stratonice*,[80] il y a un luxe de coloration très-ingénieux, très-cherché, très-chatoyant qui ne produit pas le moindre effet de couleur? Il y a un pavé de mosaïque d'une exactitude à désespérer un professeur de per-

---

[77] For discussions of this controversy, see especially A. Fontaine, *Les doctrines d'art en France*, and F. P. Chambers, *The History of Taste*, New York, 1932.

[78] Delécluze, *Louis David: son école et son temps*, p. 60.

[79] Jean Auguste Dominique Ingres, *Écrits sur l'art*, p. 8.

[80] Ingres' *Stratonice ou la maladie d'Antiochus* (1840) now in the Musée Condé, Chantilly.

spective."[81] Though he found this cold, bright, mannered "coloration" charming, it violated one of his cardinal principles: color as one of the chief means by which a painter endows his work with the semblance of life. He held Poussin (the father of the Academic point of view) responsible for the canonization of this fatal error. In his opinion, the seventeenth-century master deserved criticism more clearly on this score than on correctness of archeological detail. "On peut addresser au Poussin un reproche plus sérieux que celui d'avoir donné les costumes de la colonne Trajane à ses Crecs, ou d'avoir introduit des temples romains en Egypte, au temps des Pharaons: c'est d'avoir fait un abandon systématique de la couleur, si effectivement cet abandon a été aussi prémédité qu'on le dit."[82]

His intense preoccupation with this problem found outlet not only in written form but also in a conversation with a close friend, Baron Rivet, who reported that Delacroix, while describing the evolution of the *Death of Sardanapalus,* had specified color in painting as the equivalent of style in literature and equally subject to the control of the intellect. "La couleur," he urged, "c'est la phrase, c'est le style. On n'est un écrivain que lorsque l'on est maître, et qu'on la fait obéir à sa pensée."[83] Since we know his admiration for Diderot, it is difficult to resist the hypothesis that he had absorbed an idea that figures in Diderot's Salon of 1761 where a similar analogy between painting and literature was sustained: "La couleur est dans un tableau ce que le style est dans un morceau de littérature. Il y a des auteurs qui pensent; il y a des peintres qui ont de l'idée . . . mais de tous les temps le style et la couleur ont été des choses précieuses et rares."[84] The spontaneous reappearance of this sentiment in the course of a friendly dialogue demonstrates how deeply influential knowledge gained from reading had become in his thought.

Another conception of the function of color in which he shows links with the past appeared when, in 1852, he asserted that "la

[81] George Sand, "Impressions et souvenirs," *Œuvres complètes de George Sand,* Paris, 1873, LV, p. 77.

[82] From the article, "Poussin," which appeared in the *Moniteur universel,* June 26, 29 and 30, 1853; see *Œuvres littéraires,* II, p. 96.

[83] From an unpublished article by Baron Rivet destined for the *Revue des Deux-Mondes;* quoted by Piron, *Eugène Delacroix: sa vie et ses œuvres,* Paris, 1865, p. 70.

[84] *Œuvres complètes de Diderot,* X, p. 127.

couleur donne l'apparence de la vie."[85] Throughout the history of art theory, writers rarely failed to note this advantage. Plutarch praised its enhancement of the illusion of reality, declaring that "just as in pictures, color is more stimulating than line-drawing because it is life-like, and creates an illusion."[86] The Renaissance revived this argument. Lodovico Dolce, for one, recited a list of ancient painters — Parrhasius, Apelles, and Zeuxis — who utilized color in order to heighten the sense of reality in their works: "Cela montre la grande attention qu'avoient les anciens à bien colorer, afinque leurs ouvrages imitassent le vrai."[87] Roger de Piles established one more link in the chain of tradition in the *Cours de peinture par principes*, claiming that "la couleur est ce que rend les objets sensibles à la vûë. Et le Coloris est une des parties essentielles de la Peinture, par laquelle le Peintre sçait imiter les apparences des couleurs de tous les objets naturels, et distribuer aux objets artificiels la couleur qui leur est la plus avantageuse pour tromper la vûë."[88] And Diderot, in the *Essais sur le peinture*, endeavored to formulate a definitive statement on the issue of color versus line that would prescribe the fundamental function and value of each element. In this scheme, color, in the traditional manner, served to animate the inert forms fixed by line: "C'est le dessin qui donne la forme aux êtres; c'est la couleur qui leur donne la vie. Voilà le souffle divin qui les anime."[89] How closely, not only in sentiment but in terminology, this statement anticipates Delacroix's repetition of this theme ("la couleur donne l'apparence de la vie")!

Yet another time-honored attribute of color — its unifying power — found its way into Delacroix's thought. In the course of a lengthy comparison of the art of Poussin and Lesueur, he deplored in Poussin's paintings "cette absence d'unité, de fondu, d'effet, qui se trouvent dans Lesueur et dans tous les coloristes."[90] In so doing, he echoed the idea of that earlier champion of color, Roger de Piles, who, in his *Dialogue sur le coloris*, made one of the protago-

[85] *Journal*, I, p. 459 (February 23, 1852).

[86] Plutarch, "How the Young Man Should Study Poetry," *Moralia*, tr. F. C. Babbitt, London, 1927, I, p. 83.

[87] Dolce, *Dialogue sur la peinture, intitulé l'Aretin*, p. 217.

[88] De Piles, *Cours de peinture par principes*, p. 303.

[89] Diderot, *Essais sur la peinture*, p. 43.

[90] *Journal*, I, p. 439 (June 6, 1851).

nists of the piece, Pamphile, establish the unifying power of this element: ". . . ne sçavez-vous pas que vous détruisez le tout si vous en retranchez une partie, principalement quand elle est aussi essentielle à son tout, comme est celle du Coloris à l'Art de Peinture."[91]

Delacroix departed from the mainstream of traditional conceptions of the function of color when he specified the faculty in the spectator that was to be stimulated by means of color. He rejected disdainfully the oft-repeated idea that color should speak to the physical eye in charmingly sensuous terms. "La couleur," he declared, "n'est rien si elle n'est convenable au sujet, et si elle n'augmente pas l'effet du tableau par l'imagination. Que les Boucher et les Vanloo fassent des tons légers et charmants à l'œil, etc."[92] On this occasion, he aligned himself with the Davidian enemy camp, placing in disrepute the frivolous and sensuous courtly art of the eighteenth century in which color had played a major role.

In the seventeenth century, the French Academy had viewed color with suspicion derived from the easy appeal of color to the physical eye rather than to the intellect.[93] De Piles, foreshadowing developments in the next century, took the opposite view and seized upon this seductive power as one of the most potent weapons in the painter's technical arsenal. "Le premier soin du Peintre, aussi-bien que du Musicien, doit donc être de rendre l'entrée de ces portes [eyes and ears] libre et agréable par la force de leur harmonie, l'un dans le coloris accompagné de son clair-obscur, et l'autre dans ses accords."[94] In his view, painting was no longer to direct all its resources towards an appeal to the mind; rather, it should be content to seduce the eye alone: "Il faut donc conclure, que plus la Peinture imite fortement et fidellement la nature, plus elle nous conduit rapidement et directement vers sa fin, qui est de séduire nos yeux. . . ."[95] Thus he prepared the way for the art of Watteau, Boucher, and Fragonard, whose fragile, delicately tinted works appealed so powerfully to the aristocratic taste of the eighteenth century.

For once, Delacroix, who usually found de Piles' ideas con-

[91] De Piles, *Dialogue sur le coloris*, pp. 9-10.
[92] *Journal*, II, p. 1 (January 2, 1853).
[93] See Fontaine, *Les doctrines d'art en France*, p. 67.
[94] De Piles, *Cours de peinture par principes*, p. 9.
[95] *Ibid.*, p. 3.

genial, adopted a position closer to that of the Academy. He rejected the notion that painting possesses merely sensuous appeal. Like the Academy, he endowed it with a more profound and serious purpose. But, on the other hand, he rejected Academic subordination of color, which he considered the most persuasive factor in painting. Furthermore, this persuasive power was to be utilized to appeal to a new center of reception, the Romantic imagination, in place of the Academic intellect. In his notes for the projected *Dictionnaire*, we discover the following item: "*Couleur*: De sa supériorité ou de son exquisivité, si l'on veut, sous le rapport de l'effet sur l'imagination."[96]

By assigning to color a major role in the rendering of Romantic content he thus assumed a progressive position in relation to the schools of David and Ingres. Even so, this typically Romantic attitude was not without anticipation in the history of art theory, for as early as 1699 the theoretician, Dupuy du Grez, in his *Traité sur la peinture*, had suggested that color appealed to the imagination, declaring that "le Dessein frappe la raison et les yeux: comme le Coloris touche les yeux et l'imagination."[97]

It is abundantly clear, then, that Delacroix, rebelling against Neo-Classical emphasis on linearity, frequently resorted to past authority in order to justify a revival of color as the primary factor in painting. For the analogy between color and literary style he appears indebted, as so often before, to the example of Diderot. The writings of Dolce, de Piles, and Diderot were among the many works that included descriptions of the life-giving qualities of color. De Piles, furthermore, had already alluded to color as a unifying agent in painting. Finally, he revived the old issue of the function of color in regard to the end of painting and abandoned the Academic conception in favor of the progressive view of color as a primary means of enabling Romantic content to stir the spectator's imagination.

LINE

This firm insistence on the primacy of color over line does not

---

[96] *Journal*, III, p. 56 (January 25, 1857). For the possible influence of scientific theories of color on Delacroix's thought, see Johnson, *Delacroix*, pp. 64-72.

[97] Bernard Dupuy du Grez, *Traité sur la peinture pour en apprendre la téorie et se perfectionner dans la pratique*, Toulouse, 1699, p. 208.

mean, however, that Delacroix was unaware of the importance of line. Arch-colorist that he was, he nevertheless accused Titian of a failure to realize the charm that resides in line: "Est-ce que l'espèce de froideur que j'ai toujours sentie pour le Titien ne viendrait pas de l'ignorance presque constante où il est relativement au charme des lignes?"[98] As we shall discover, he attempted to evolve a new concept of line — a concept that might be termed painterly line.

In part, his rejection of the linearism of David and Ingres stemmed from his desire to base his art on a fundamental adherence to natural appearances. Where, he inquired, in a passage which clearly foreshadows Impressionist attitudes, does nature present the firmly contoured forms of the Neo-Classicists? "Je suis à ma fenêtre," he wrote, "et je vois le plus beau paysage: l'idée d'une ligne ne me vient pas à l'esprit. L'alouette chante, la rivière réfléchit mille diamants, le feuillage murmure; où sont les lignes qui produisent ces charmantes sensations?"[99] In practice he had achieved these charming, linearless sensations in a work of the 1840's, *Landscape at Champrosay* (Fig. 36).[100] All the elements of this landscape fuse into an atmospheric whole — a fusion engineered by the exploitation of soft, broad brushstrokes that operate freely across the surface of the canvas unhindered by any restrictive contour lines. Stylistically, it shows seeds of that alleged formlessness which hostile critics would later profess to see in Impressionist landscapes.

The artificial nature of linearity was already indicated by Lodovico Dolce who, in opposition to Florentine predilection for line, advised his readers that "il faut que le mélange des couleurs soit tempéré, et mélangé de manière, qu'il représente le naturel, et qu'il ne reste rien qui blesse la vûe, telles que sont les lignes des contours qu'on doit éviter, parce que la nature ne les marque point. . . ."[101]

[98] *Journal*, I, p. 202 (March 7, 1847). It is worth noting that even that staunch supporter of color, de Piles, had been careful to give line its due: "Il [drawing] est la clef des Beaux-Arts; c'est luy qui donne entrée aux autres parties de la Peinture; c'est l'organe de nos pensées, l'instrument de nos démonstrations, et la lumière de nôtre entendement." De Piles, *op.cit.*, p. 127.

[99] *Journal*, I, p. 299 (July 15, 1849).

[100] Champrosay was the village near Fontainebleau where Delacroix maintained a retreat and the place where he recorded his characterization of lines in nature. See Huyghe, *Delacroix*, pls. 24-25, for photographs of Delacroix's house there.

[101] Dolce, *Dialogue sur la peinture, intitulé l'Aretin*, p. 221.

In order to reinforce his argument against the linearists, Delacroix attacked the frequently sponsored conception of line as an essential ingredient of beauty. For those critics who maintained such a position he had nothing but scorn: "Ce fameux beau que les uns voient dans la ligne serpentine, les autres dans la ligne droite, ils se sont tous obstinés à ne le jamais voir que dans les lignes. . . . Ils ne veulent voir proportion, harmonie, qu'entre des lignes: le reste pour eux est chaos, et le compas seul est juge."[102]

Among those writers who had suggested the adoption of the serpentine line was Giovanni Paolo Lomazzo, the Mannerist theorist, who in 1584 decreed that "straight lines and sharp angles should always be avoided" ("lasciandone sempre indi le linee rette, e gli angoli acuti . . .").[103] Probably as a result of Lomazzo's popularity in France, this preference for curvilinear line appears in the *De arte graphica* of Du Fresnoy, who declared that "les parties doivent avoir leurs contours en ondes, et ressembler en cela à la flâme, ou au serpent lorsqu'il rampe sur la terre."[104] The specific connection between beauty and the serpentine line, however, was made by William Hogarth in the *Analysis of Beauty* of 1753. One is tempted to conjecture that Delacroix had in mind the words of Hogarth when referring to this concept since he was familiar, if not with his writings, at least with the nature of his art.[105] In Hogarth's scheme, the serpentine quality of an undulating, curvilinear line constituted the very essence of beauty. In a famous passage of the *Analysis of Beauty* he maintained that "the eye hath this sort of enjoyment in winding walks, and serpentine rivers, and all sorts of objects, whose forms, as we shall see hereafter, are composed principally of what, I call, the *waving* and *serpentine* lines. Intricacy in form, therefore, I shall define to be that peculiarity in

---

[102] *Journal*, I, p. 299 (July 15, 1849).

[103] From Giovanni Paolo Lomazzo's *Treatise on the Art of Painting*, tr. R. Haydock, Oxford, 1598, in Elizabeth Holt, *A Documentary History of Art*, Princeton, 1947, p. 263. The Italian is from Gio. Paolo Lomazzo, *Trattato dell'arte della pittura, scultura, ed architettura*, Rome, 1844, II, p. 97. Leonardo, too, had been aware of the serpentine quality of line: "The contours of any object should be considered with the most careful attention, observing how they twist like a serpent. These serpentine curves are to be studied to see whether they turn as parts of a round curvature or are of an angular concavity." Leonardo da Vinci, *Treatise on Painting*, I, p. 64.

[104] Du Fresnoy, *L'Art de peinture*, p. 19.

[105] For references to Hogarth's achievement in art, see the *Journal*, II, pp. 339 and 341 (June 17, 1855).

the lines, which compose it, that *leads the eye a wanton kind of chace*, and from the pleasure that gives the mind, intitles it to the name of beautiful."[106]

In his refutation of Hogarth's enticing formula, Delacroix had substantial support in the writings of Diderot who, in a similarly scornful manner, denounced all sorts of curvilinear devices. In the *Pensées détachées*, under the heading "De la beauté," he insisted that "tout ce que l'on dit des lignes elliptiques, circulaires, serpentines, ondoyantes, est absurde."[107] Such strong terms would have been extremely congenial to the Romantic painter.

Further motivation for his rejection of serpentine line may be discerned in a quotation he culled from Poussin's writings. Poussin, as reported by Giovanni Pietro Bellori, had prescribed the following rule for the judicious use of line: "The design of the objects . . . should be of a similar nature as are the expressions for the concepts of these same objects. The structure or composition of the parts should not be laboriously studied, nor *recherché*, nor labored, but true to nature."[108] Delacroix paraphrased this passage in the following manner: "Il faut, dit-il [Poussin], que le dessin tourne toujours au profit de la pensée: le dessin ni la composition de toutes les parties ne doit point être recherché, ni étudié, ni trop élaboré, mais conforme en tout à la nature du sujet."[109]

Poussin's appeal for a reaction against the involved, labored, and elaborate drawing of the Mannerists elicited a sympathetic response from Delacroix, who opposed what he considered the equally mannered styles of both the Rococo period and the school of Ingres. Hence, no doubt, the relative sobriety of many of his drawings, which often suppress a display of technical flourish for its own sake. Consider, for example, the preparatory sketch for *Jacob Wrestling with the Angel* (Fig. 37). Here technique, while abundantly expressive, bows to the dictates of naturalness and the

106 William Hogarth, *The Analysis of Beauty*, ed. Joseph Burke, Oxford, 1955, p. 42. (1st ed., 1753.)

107 Diderot, "Pensées détachées," *Essais sur la peinture*, p. 196.

108 Poussin, "Observations on Painting," p. 368. Anthony Blunt has suggested that most of the matter contained in the section entitled "Di alcune forme della maniera magnifica," of which the quoted passage is a part, constitutes a reading note by Poussin from Agostino Mascardi's *Dell'arte historica*, Rome, 1636. See Blunt, "Poussin's Notes on Painting," p. 346.

109 From the article on Poussin; see *Œuvres littéraires*, II, p. 93.

nature of the content. For nowhere do the heavy, blunt pencil strokes emerge as brilliant entities to be admired for their own sake; they serve instead to establish the gnarled, tortured quality of the trees which seem to respond sympathetically to the struggle of the antagonists. Or, by the modest means of simple, vertical hatchings, they render the softer bulk of the mountains in the background. And, with a notable indifference to legible detail, they outline and enliven the pulsating, intertwined forms involved in cosmic combat.

This sketch also serves to introduce another aspect of Delacroix's conception of the proper function of line. For, in addition to avoidance of overt virtuosity, it manifests a fundamentally painterly quality — the result of a lack of linear clarity that is evident especially in the foreground where an almost liquid fusion of elements evokes the technique of the brush rather than the technique of pencil.

The painterly quality achieved here in the linear realm of drawing assumes an even greater emphasis, of course, in actual paintings. In conversations with assistants and friends he was very articulate on this point. Louis de Planet, for example, reported that "M. Delacroix préfère dans les retouches . . . qu'un contour soit tout à fait confondu avec le milieu qu'on a placé pour retoucher. . . ."[110] This precept, pregnant with significance for the imminent development of Impressionism, finds a visual counterpart in a host of mature works. In a very late example, *Tobias and the Angel* of 1863 (Fig. 24), all firm contours dissolve. Figures and objects emerge only reluctantly from the pulsating, electric network of brushstrokes which serve, at the same time, to suggest some intervening veil of atmosphere between solid masses.

During an exchange of views with Chopin (recorded by George Sand), Delacroix firmly defended his attitude towards line. Anticipating from Chopin the standard argument in favor of line, he exclaimed: "Attendez! Chopin, je sais ce que vous allez dire: le contour est ce qui empêche les objets de se confondre les uns avec les autres; mais la nature est sobre de contours arrêtés. La lumière qui est sa vie, son mode d'existence, brise à chaque instant les silhouettes

[110] Planet, *Souvenirs de travaux de peinture avec M. Eugène Delacroix*, p. 43. According to Planet, this advice was rendered by Delacroix on Monday, November 8, 1841.

et, au lieu de dessiner à plat, elle enlève tout en ronde bosse."[111]

In both theory and practice, then, Delacroix endeavored to avoid the hard, dry, firm contours of Neo-Classicism. For authority in this painterly problem, he turned to the writings of Sir Joshua Reynolds. In the Journal entry of January 11, 1857, under the heading *Pinceau*, we find: "Beau pinceau. Reynolds disait qu'un peintre devait dessiner avec le pinceau."[112] The source of this paraphrase of Reynolds' counsel occurs in the Second Discourse, which stated: "What, therefore, I wish to impress upon you is, that whenever an opportunity offers, you paint your studies instead of drawing them."[113]

The evolution of Delacroix's conception of line, one may conclude, was influenced by a number of authorities: Like Lodovico Dolce, he found no evidence in nature for the existence of firm, opaque contour. As part of his reaction against the "mannered" drawing of both the Rococo and Ingres, he cited the example of Poussin, who favored a sober conformity of line to the rule of thought and of nature. Rather surprisingly, for an artist who often revived the dynamic, curvilinear patterns of the Baroque style, he rejected the primacy of serpentine line — especially as a factor in the attainment of beauty in the Hogarthian sense. Diderot, in this matter, had already furnished a precedent by referring to all such theories as absurd. Finally, as support for the type of painterly drawing he had already achieved in both sketches and paintings, he paraphrased Sir Joshua Reynolds' appeal for painted rather than drawn sketches.

[111] Sand, *Impressions et souvenirs*, pp. 83-84.
[112] *Journal*, III, p. 10.
[113] *Sir Joshua Reynolds: Discourses on Art*, p. 34.

CONCLUSION

THAT IMPLACABLE FOE of Rousseauistic Romanticism, Irving Babbitt, sounded in 1919 a still popular hostility to the period that produced such towering figures as Delacroix, Berlioz, Hugo, and Wordsworth. Like subsequent critics, he founded his argument on a fundamental distrust of Romantic freedom from the rational controls characteristic of Classicial procedures. This freedom, he insisted, "means only emancipation from outer control" and would result "in the most dangerous form of anarchy — the anarchy of the imagination."[1] As this once healthy corrective to Romantic excess dims in importance, however, the undeniable luster of the Romantic achievement retains its brilliance. Quite apart from the extraordinary productions of the artistic practitioners of the movement — works that, alone, justify the Romantic aesthetic — Babbitt's criticism now rings a hollow, polemical note in the light of Delacroix's lifelong struggle to transform the anarchy of the imagination into a lucid yet vital creative instrument. Not only the content of his ideas on art but even the method by which he cited, adopted, modified and absorbed previous art theory testifies to this serious, exalted aim.

We have discovered how extraordinarily heavy was his debt to past theory. Moreover, analysis of his method and purpose has revealed certain practical and psychological motivations for this unusual erudition. As a result, the problem of the nature of his Romanticism assumes clearer focus. In his case, at least, Babbitt's picture of an extravagant, irresponsible Romantic throwing rational discretion to the winds does not apply. In both his theory and his art Delacroix endeavored to solve the problem that confronts every artist, whether born into a Classical or Romantic ambience, namely

---

[1] Irving Babbitt, *Rousseau and Romanticism*, New York, 1955, p. 286. (1st ed., 1919.) Babbitt's hostile attitude was anticipated by Pierre Lasserre in an influential work, *Le romantisme français*, Paris, 1907. For a useful survey of reactions to the Romantic period, see Rudrauf, *Eugène Delacroix et le problème du romantisme artistique*, pp. 12-32.

the proper relationship of the rational and irrational forces of the artistic personality during the genesis of a work of art.

The extent of his acquaintance with antecedent art theory has been established in breadth and in depth: During the course of this study we have noted his knowledge of the ideas of writers on art and literature extending from Longinus to Baudelaire with the examples of Leonardo da Vinci, Lodovico Dolce, Benvenuto Cellini, Poussin, La Rochefoucauld, Boileau, Roger de Piles, Addison, Reynolds, Voltaire, Diderot, Madame de Staël, and Byron assuming special relevance as sources of information. This extensive galaxy of names is surpassed only by the formidable range of theoretical subject matter. Always preoccupied with aesthetic problems and, after 1857, compiling data for the projected *Dictionnaire des Beaux-Arts*, he managed to acquire considerable erudition concerning the aim of art, the imitation of nature, the creative process, beauty, regularity, unity, color, and line. Under these categories, subsidiary topics such as the sublime, imagination, and genius enrich the general texture of ideas so that, taken as a whole, the range of Delacroix's theory comes close to embracing the full repertory of topics treated in the history of art theory. In this manner, he was armed with a comprehensive arsenal of concepts which served either to reinforce his adoption of traditional ideas or to justify his exploitation of more revolutionary ones.

This frequent borrowing from the rich treasure of the past occurs in his writings in three basic forms — as direct quotations from past writers, who are frequently but not always identified; as paraphrases of ideas that will appear familiar only to one who is conversant with his sources; and, finally, as more or less assimilated material in his own ostensibly original thought. As a result, his art theory takes on the quality of a subtle mixture of traditional and original ideas, with the emphasis on the former.

To characterize Delacroix's theory as heavily dependent on the past in no way, however, removes that theory from its close relationship to his art. Even the bare and unidentified notation of an idea, culled from a favorite author and unadorned by any commentary, constitutes concrete evidence for the artist's preoccupation with that idea at a certain period in his life. Happily, his commitment to that

1. *Orpheus Bringing Civilization to the Primitive Greeks.* 1843-47.
Library, Palais Bourbon, Paris

2. *Attila and His Hordes Overrun Italy and the Arts.* 1843-47.
Library, Palais Bourbon, Paris

3. Gustave Courbet. *Bathers*. 1853. Fabre Museum, Montpellier

4. *Jacob Wrestling with the Angel.* 1854-61. Chapel of the Holy Angels,
Church of Saint-Sulpice, Paris

5. *Dante and Virgil.* 1822. Louvre, Paris

6. *The Death of Sardanapalus.* 1827. Louvre, Paris

7. *The Massacre at Chios.* 1824. Louvre, Paris

8. *Heliodorus Driven from the Temple.* 1854-61. Chapel of the Holy Angels,
Church of Saint-Sulpice, Paris

9. *Lion Mauling a Dead Arab*. 1847. National Gallery, Oslo

10. *Indian Woman Gnawed by a Tiger*. 1852. Private Collection

11. *Seated Nude: Mademoiselle Rose.* 1821-23. Louvre, Paris

TEIKYO WESTMAR UNIVERSITY

Thurs
12:00
S.U.

Gail V.
Eileen A.
Todd J.
Jerri J.
Gary J.
Chris R.
Jodie S.

1002 3rd Avenue S.E. • LeMars, Iowa 51031
(712) 546-7081, Fax # 546-4061

12. Study of a detail for the decoration of the Salon of Peace,
Hôtel de Ville, Paris (destroyed by fire, 1871). 1852-54.
Louvre, Paris

13. *Study of an Algerian Interior.* 1832. Louvre, Paris

14. *Studies of Arab Women.* 1832. Louvre, Paris

15. *Algerian Women in Their Apartment.* 1834. Louvre, Paris

16. *Algerian Women in Their Apartment.* 1849.
Fabre Museum, Montpellier

17. *The Abduction of Rebecca*. 1859. Louvre, Paris

18. *Arab Women at a Fountain*. 1832. Louvre, Paris

19. *Studies of Antique Coins.* 1825.
Louvre, Paris

20. *The Rhône.* 1833-38. Salon of
the King, Palais Bourbon, Paris

21. *Lion Hunt.* 1861. Chicago Art Institute (Potter Palmer Collection)

22. Peter Paul Rubens. *Lion Hunt.* 1616-17. Alte Pinakothek, Munich

23. Execution of Marino Faliero. 1826.
Wallace Collection, London

24. Tobias and the Angel. 1863.
Reinhart Collection, Winterthur

25. *Boissy d'Anglas at the Convention.* 1831. Bordeaux Museum

26. *St. George and the Dragon.* 1847. Louvre, Paris

27. Painted sketch for the *Lion Hunt*. Ca. 1854. Private Collection, France

28. *Lion Hunt*. 1855. Bordeaux Museum

29. *Christ in the Garden of Gethsemane.* 1826. Church of
Saint-Paul-Saint-Louis, Paris

30. *The Natchez.* Salon of 1835. Lord and Lady Walston
Collection, Newton Hall, Cambridge

31. *Medea*. 1862. Louvre, Paris

32. *Entombment*. 1848. Museum of Fine Arts, Boston

33. *Sea at Dieppe.* 1852. Marcel Beurdeley Collection, Paris

34. Claude Monet, *Impression: Rising Sun.* 1872.
Marmottan Museum, Paris

35. Vincent Van Gogh, *Crows over the Wheatfield.* 1890. Collection
V. W. Van Gogh, Laren

36. *Landscape at Champrosay.* 1842. Private Collection, Paris

37. Study for *Jacob Wrestling with the Angel*. 1854-61. Private Collection

idea is frequently verified by its appearance in another context in a completely assimilated guise.

What reasons have come to light to explain the nature and extent of Delacroix's interest in prior art theory? What possible motivating forces compelled him to rely so heavily upon support from the past? In the first place, he possessed, as his writings so eloquently witness, a keen intellect that both relished and required acquaintanceship with various solutions to the fundamental problems of art theory. Many of these solutions were to have been incorporated into the *Dictionnaire*. The significance of this interest extends, however, beyond the pleasures and needs of intellectual inquiry. The emergent pattern of his investigations suggests certain general characteristics of purpose that are of some import for the nature of his total aesthetic as well as the nature of his art.

This pattern sheds some light on the motivating force that compelled him to devote so much of his theoretical notation and analysis to Classical theory. It has been pointed out that the mantle of leader of the Romantic Movement caused him discomfort. He was extremely sensitive (especially in his mature years) to any attempt to identify him as a full-fledged Romantic personality. In a letter to his friend Madame Cavé, he dissociated himself from any conception of a Romantic school, claiming that "le mot d'école ne signifie rien; le vrai dans les arts est relatif à la personne seule qui écrit, peint, compose dans quelque genre que ce soit: le vrai que je dégagerai dans la nature, n'est pas celui qui frappera tel autre peintre, mon élève ou non: par conséquent on ne peut transmettre le sentiment du beau et du vrai et l'expression: *faire école*, ne contient qu'une absurdité. . . ."[2] And we have noted his sharp reaction ("Je suis un pur classique!") when a misguided admirer suggested that he was the Victor Hugo of painting.[3] Undoubtedly hyperbolic in nature, this retort nevertheless dramatizes that aspect of his personality which sought identification with the predominantly Classical French tradition of painting and which compelled him to seek obstinately the honor of membership in the Academy — an honor finally accorded in 1857 after many years of disappointment. It also reflects more subtle motives for his cultivation of Classicism.

[2] *Correspondance générale*, III, p. 265.
[3] Related by Paul Jamot, "Delacroix," p. 101.

CONCLUSION

We have observed his tendency to regard the Antique not only in its Neo-Classical guise as something cold, restrained, and measured in artistic expression but also in its Dionysiac form, throbbing with dynamic vitality. This dual conception of the Antique is, in turn, symbolic of his refusal to consider the Romantic and Classical modes of expression as mutually exclusive. He rejected the traditional categorizing of great artists as Classical or Romantic. Like Stendhal, he considered Racine to be "un romantique pour les gens de son temps."[4] And, in Mozart, he discerned more than a mere model of Classical perfection. After attending a performance of *Don Giovanni,* in 1847, he exclaimed: "Quel chef-d'œuvre de romantisme! Et cela en 1785!"[5] Similarly, in the realm of art theory, he discovered in antecedent, non-Romantic periods ample justification for the progressive and Romantic elements of his art.

The same respect for the great tradition of French painting that motivated his persistent attempts to enter the Academy no doubt inspired, in part, this tendency to cite Classical theory in order to justify certain aspects of his anti-Classical expression. In Boileau, he found confirmation of the necessity for a realistic basis of art. Inspiration for the exploitation of sketchlike technique for greater brilliance of effect (a sentiment also advocated by the more contemporary Byron) was available to him in a passage culled from the pages of La Rochefoucauld. His oft repeated conception of unfinish as a means of stimulating the spectator's imagination could be found in works he knew by de Piles and Diderot. For a discussion of the role of irregularity, he selected a passage from the works of Edgar Allan Poe which, while advocating irregularity as a necessary

[4] *Journal,* III, p. 23 (January 13, 1857). Stendhal in 1823 had already suggested that Racine was a Romantic: "Je n'hésite pas à avancer que Racine a été romantique; il a donné, aux marquis de la cour de Louis XIV, une peinture des passions, tempérée par l'*extrème dignité* qui alors était de mode . . ." Stendhal (Marie Henri Beyle), "Racine et Shakespeare," *Œuvres complètes de Stendhal,* Paris, 1925, I, p. 40. Initially hostile to Stendhal's ideas, Delacroix ultimately became a friend and admirer of the writer, who is mentioned frequently in the Journal. Margaret Gilman (in *Baudelaire the Critic,* p. 40) has pointed out the interrelationship of the ideas of Diderot, Stendhal, and Delacroix: "The opinions of the three, dissimilar in some respects, agree in others. Moreover, Stendhal was a reader and admirer of Diderot as was Delacroix of both Diderot and Stendhal; so that there is a whole cross-play of influences at work."

[5] *Journal,* I, p. 185 (February 9, 1847).

component of beauty, cited a seventeenth-century source — Francis Bacon — as authority.

Further motivation for his frequent forays into past theory stemmed from his desire to curb what he considered the excessively Romantic aspect of his temperament by adherence to Classical ideals of restraint. This conscious control of his emotions was also evident in his everyday conduct. He preferred to observe a strict and orderly regime (necessitated in part by delicate health), and his social conduct was famous for high standards of elegant deportment that contrasted sharply with bohemian behavior. Baudelaire tells us that "au premier coup d'œil, Eugène Delacroix apparaissait simplement comme un homme *éclairé* dans le sens honorable du mot, comme un parfait *gentleman* sans préjugés et sans passions. Ce n'était que par une fréquentation plus assidue qu'on pouvait pénétrer sous le vernis et deviner les parties abstruses de son âme."[6]

The predilection for discipline and order that characterized his nonartistic personality also found expression in his dependence upon Classical theories of artistic creation. As early as 1824, when his youthful ardor and enthusiasm were extremely intense, he felt the need to balance strong emotional tendencies by the cultivation of rational powers: "Ce qui me fait plaisir, c'est que j'acquiers de la raison, sans perdre l'émotion excitée par le beau."[7] And twenty-three years later, in 1847, he still maintained the concept of the reconciliation of passion and reason as the only feasible means of artistic creation: "Le peintre a bien cette première vue passionnée sur son sujet. Mais cet essai de lui-même est plus informe que celui du comédien. Plus il aura de talent, plus le calme de l'étude ajoutera de beautés, non pas en se conformant le plus exactement possible à sa première idée, mais en la secondant par la chaleur de son exécution."[8] Therefore, one discovers without surprise that he

---

6 Baudelaire, "L'Œuvre et la vie d'Eugène Delacroix," p. 438.

7 *Journal*, I, p. 53 (February 27, 1824).

8 *Journal*, I, p. 174 (January 27, 1847). Maxime du Camp, who knew Delacroix at this period ("Lorsque je connus Delacroix, il avait cinquante ans . . ."), records the painter's excitability and need for restraint and control while painting a small *Fantasia*: "Il peignait une *Fantasia* de petite dimension . . . Delacroix était très animé. Il soufflait bruyamment; son pinceau devenait d'une agilité surprenante. La main du cavalier grandissait, grandissait, elle était déjà plus grosse que la tête et prenait des proportions telles, que je m'écriai: 'Mais, mon cher maître, que faites-vous?' Delacroix jeta un cri de saisissement, comme si je l'eusse réveillé en sursaut; il me dit: 'Il fait trop chaud ici, je deviens

examined Classical art theory not only for those elements that justified the Romantic characteristics of his own art but also for the traditional principles of Classical procedure that might aid in restraining and shaping the disordered mode of expression that a temperament of strong emotional impulse tends to encourage. Hence his profound and continuous interest in unity, order, regularity, measure, and harmony as expressed in Classical art. These visible attributes of the exercise of reason and judgment appealed to him since they provided the means by which he might impart intellectual clarity to the dark, nebulous content of his art. And, once incorporated into his art, they no doubt relieved the burden of criticism such as that of Delécluze who eagerly indicated his lapse from Classical canons of taste and form.

How, then, is this subtle blend of old and new theory, of Classical and Romantic attitudes, related to traditional conceptions of Delacroix's Romanticism? We have already noted the opinions of Théophile Gautier and Frédéric Villot who held that his art theory was utterly opposed to his artistic practice. On the basis of Delacroix's preoccupation with such factors as line, color, unity, the sketch — all matters intimately involved with the physical nature of painting — this alleged barrier seems to disappear. Moreover, we have discovered a close interrelationship between the Classical and the Romantic aspects of his theory and a constant application of now one, now the other, often the two mingled, to his visual expression. As a result, it is difficult to accept the view that he schizophrenically exploited one attitude in theory and another in practice.

The seemingly alien burden of Classical content in his thought constitutes an integral part of his Herculean attempt to reconcile the rational and the irrational, the Classical and the Romantic. That is why one must question Raymond Escholier's dismissal of Delacroix's theory as of negligible importance for the development of his Romantic expression. Equally questionable is his attribution of Delacroix's interest in Classical principles to the sobering influence of old age. For, although the exuberant and preponderant

---

fou.' Puis il prit son couteau à palette et enleva la main. Il avait l'air farouche; machinalement il fit quelques frottis sur les terrains, comme pour se calmer. 'La nuit vient, me dit-il; voulez-vous que nous sortions?' " *Souvenirs littéraires de Maxime du Camp, 1822-1894*, p. 271.

CONCLUSION

Romanticism expressed in such youthful works as *Massacre at Chios* (1824), *Death of Sardanapalus* (1827) and *Boissy d'Anglas at the Convention* (1831) was tempered by a more thoughtful approach in many later works (especially the monumental decorations of official buildings in Paris), it is also evident that, already in the 1820's, he endeavored to curb his ardent temperament by a commitment to reason. And this cultivation of reason was coupled with an interest in Antique style as manifested in Greek coins and statuary[9] — an interest expressed in painting as early as 1821 in the representations of the *Four Seasons* executed for installation in the dining room of the actor Talma.[10] His profound investigation of Classical theory (as well as Classical art) cannot be attributed to age; it is, rather, an intensification of a preoccupation already evident in the midst of his early, predominantly Romantic years.

In like manner, Lionello Venturi's theory which attributed to the Classical aspects of Delacroix's aesthetic his failure to achieve a pure, hence desirable, state of Romantic expression must be abandoned. Certainly we have abundant proof that a reprehensible desire to pay obeisance to attitudes officially and socially approved never lay at the foundation of Delacroix's effort. There is no reason to assume that in the private medium of his Journal he felt compelled to manufacture a false, classicizing façade. He had, rather, ample reason for a sincere investigation of the principles of Classical art and theory. The result may lack the purity of an unmixed substance and pose problems for those critics who champion revolt and progress as the sure tokens of genius. On the basis of the evidence provided by his writings, however, Delacroix's motivation appears irreproachable.

Fundamentally, the attitudes of Escholier and Venturi must be rejected because Delacroix, practiced in the act of artistic creation, realized that the gulf between the Romantic and the Classical modes of expression was not the unbridgeable one pictured by writers who have sought to isolate the two as opposing forces. In his view, Romantic aims could be furthered by Classical procedures just as Classical expression could benefit by an infusion of Romantic warmth and brio. In his own case, the priority of the Romantic

9 See above, p. 68 and nn. 71 and 72.
10 See Johnson, "Delacroix's Decorations for Talma's Dining Room," esp. pp. 85-86.

principle is clear. He conceives of art as subjective expression — as the means of soul to soul communication. The imagination plays a vital role in the creative process both on the part of the artist and the spectator. In order to involve the spectator's imagination in the creative process he cultivates a sketchlike technique in his finished pictures, relying upon the imaginative power of the spectator to supply what the artist has purposely withheld. Not without a certain lack of modesty (a quality he held in disesteem), he gladly embraced the traditional concept of the natural genius whose flaws and inequalities are made palatable by the frequent achievement of the sublime. As a corollary to this conception of the genius he adopts a position on the question of rules that is firmly opposed to any restriction of the creative spirit. He rejects the Classical quality of regularity as a requisite for beauty. And, favoring boldness in technique and approach, he exalts color as a primary purveyor of subjective expression.

In Classical theory he uncovered ideas that did not contradict this Romantic program. Instead he found solace and aid — solace in the fact that many of the progressive and Romantic tendencies of his own art were fully justified by those Classical authorities invoked by his Neo-Classical critics and aid in the traditionally Classical principles of unity, order, measure, and form that could be utilized to alleviate the Romantic invitation to formlessness and incoherence — qualities that would have hindered the immediate communication that was his primary object in art.

His constant utilization of Classical theory was in no way spurious. Equipped with a liberal and profound intellect, he adopted a dual approach to aesthetic problems. In an age noted for rigid adherence to dogmatic positions, he appreciated both sides of the creative coin — the rational and the irrational. By nature, temperament, and historical circumstance he was committed to the progressive and vital mode of Romantic expression. Yet, he recognized the pitfalls that lay in that direction. In Classical theory he discovered unexpected inspiration for the exploitation of irrational content in his art. Of equal importance was the more traditional aspect of Classicism which provided the tools and weapons forged by the powers of intellect and judgment to harness the dark powers of nonreason, i.e., to bring order to the incipient anarchy of the Romantic imagination.

Delacroix, then, was a tempered Romantic. In a sense, his mission was to reintegrate reason and emotion, to heal the breach between these indispensable modes of existence which had opened already, according to Francis Fergusson, in the seventeenth century.[11] In a period prone to embrace too willingly the irrational approach he sounded a call to order. It is this heroic attempt to establish a balance between these two poles that makes his theory historically and intellectually valid. Moreover, it is the tension generated by this polar stretch which justifies the occasional failures in his art and explains the extraordinary successes which consolidate his position as the ranking painter of the first half of the nineteenth century. Like another illustrious countryman he realized that any effective work of art is the result of a fusion of the romantic and classical propensities which reside in every individual. As André Gide puts it: "Il importe de considérer que la lutte entre classicisme et romantisme existe aussi bien à l'intérieur de chaque esprit. Et c'est de cette lutte même que doit naître l'œuvre; l'œuvre d'art classique raconte le triomphe de l'ordre et de la mesure sur le romantisme intérieur."[12]

[11] Francis Fergusson, *The Idea of a Theater*, p. 3.

[12] André Gide, "Réponse à une enquête de 'La Renaissance' sur le classicisme" (1923), *Œuvres complètes d'André Gide*, ed. L. Martin-Chauffier, Paris, 1932-39, x, p. 26. These conclusions reinforce the recent tendency to reintegrate Delacroix's artistic personality. In the words of René Huyghe (*Delacroix*, p. 56): "The endlessly resumed discussion of whether he was really romantic or classical can only be futile, for his originality consisted precisely in putting a stop to the contradiction in which those of his time were becoming bogged down. . . ."

BIBLIOGRAPHY

THE DELACROIX bibliography is of enormous proportions and I have made no attempt to encompass it here. This one is strictly limited to those sources, books, catalogues, and articles which have contributed directly to the content of this study. For more extensive bibliographies, see Lucien Rudrauf, *Eugène Delacroix et le problème du romantisme artistique*, Paris, 1942 and René Huyghe, *Delacroix*, New York, 1963.

DELACROIX'S WRITINGS

Delacroix, Eugène. *Correspondance générale d'Eugène Delacroix*, ed. André Joubin. 5 vols. 2d ed. Paris, Plon, 1936-38.

——. *Ecrits d'Eugène Delacroix*, ed. Jacques and René Wittman. 2 vols. Paris, Plon, 1942.

——. *Eugène Delacroix: Œuvres littéraires*, ed. Elie Faure. 2 vols. Paris, Les éditions G. Crès et Cie., 1923.

——. *Journal d'Eugène Delacroix*, ed. Paul Flat. 3 vols. Paris, Plon et Nourrit, 1893-95.

——. *Journal d'Eugène Delacroix*, ed. André Joubin. 3 vols. Paris, Plon, 1960.

——. *Les dangers de la cour*, ed. Jean Marchand. Avignon, 1960.

——. *Lettres d'Eugène Delacroix*, ed. Philippe Burty. Paris, Quantin, 1878.

——. *Lettres inédites d'Eugène Delacroix*, ed. J.-J. Guiffrey. Paris, Rillet et Dumoulin, 1877.

——. *Lettres intimes: correspondance inédite*, ed. Alfred Dupont. Paris, Gallimard, 1954.

——. *On Art Criticism*, tr. Walter Pach. New York, Curt Valentin, 1946.

——. *The Journal of Eugène Delacroix*, tr. Walter Pach. New York, Covici, Friede, Inc., 1937.

——. *The Journal of Eugène Delacroix*, ed. H. Wellington; tr. Lucy Norton. New York, Oxford University Press, 1951.

BIBLIOGRAPHY

CATALOGUES

Centenaire d'Eugène Delacroix: 1798-1863. Introduction by M. Sérullaz, Paris, 1963.

Delacroix. Introduction by Lorenz Eitner. The Arts Council, Great Britain. Edinburgh, Shenval Press, 1964.

Delacroix et la gravure romantique. Preface by Julien Cain. Paris, 1963.

Delacroix: ses maîtres, ses amis, ses élèves, ed. G. Martin-Méry. Bordeaux, 1963.

Eugène Delacroix: 1798-1863, ed. Lee Johnson. Toronto, 1962.

Eugène Delacroix: 1798-1863. Günter Busch *et al.* Hamburg, 1964.

Exposition Eugène Delacroix. Preface by Paul Jamot. Paris, 1930.

Mémorial de l'exposition Eugène Delacroix. Introduction by M. Sérullaz. Paris, Editions des musées nationaux, 1963.

L'Œuvre complet d'Eugène Delacroix, ed. Ernest Chesneau and Alfred Robaut. Paris, Charavay frères, 1885.

BOOKS AND ARTICLES ON DELACROIX

Badt, Kurt. *Eugène Delacroix: Drawings.* Oxford, Bruno Cassirer, 1946.

Christoffel, Ulrich. *Eugène Delacroix.* Munich, Verlag F. Bruckmann, 1951.

Dargenty, G. *Eugène Delacroix par lui-même.* Paris, J. Rouam, 1885.

Escholier, Raymond. *Delacroix: peintre, graveur, écrivain.* 3 vols. Paris, H. Floury, 1926.

Gillot, Hubert. *E. Delacroix: l'homme — ses idées — son œuvre.* Paris, Société d'édition "Les belles lettres," 1928.

Hamilton, George Heard. "Eugène Delacroix and Lord Byron," *Gazette des Beaux-Arts,* February 1943, pp. 99-110, and *ibid.,* July-December 1944, pp. 365-86.

Huyghe, René. *Delacroix.* New York, Harry N. Abrams, Inc., 1963.

———. "Delacroix et Baudelaire: A New Epoch in Art and Poetry," *Arts Yearbook 2,* 1958, pp. 27-46.

Jamot, Paul. "Delacroix," *Le romantisme et l'art.* Preface by E. Herriot. Paris, 1928, pp. 93-134.

BIBLIOGRAPHY

Johnson, Lee. *Delacroix*. London, Weidenfeld and Nicolson, 1963.

———. "Delacroix's Decorations for Talma's Dining Room," *Burlington Magazine*, XCIX, March 1957, pp. 78-89.

———. "The Formal Sources of Delacroix's 'Barque de Dante,' " *Burlington Magazine*, C, July 1958, pp. 228-32.

Lambert, Elie. " 'L'Apartement' des femmes d'Alger et les albums de voyage d'Eugène Delacroix au Maroc," *Revue de l'art*, LXV, May 1934, pp. 187-91.

Marchand, Jean. "Delacroix fut écrivain avant d'être peintre," *Les nouvelles littéraires*, August 14, 1952.

Meier-Graefe, Julius. *Eugène Delacroix: Beiträge zu einer Analyse*. Munich, R. Piper, 1913.

Moreau-Nélaton, Etienne. *Delacroix raconté par lui-même*. 2 vols. Paris, Librairie Renouard, 1916.

Mras, George P. "Literary Sources of Delacroix's Conception of the Sketch and the Imagination," *Art Bulletin*, XLIV, June 1962, pp. 103-11.

———. "*Ut Pictura Musica*: A Study of Delacroix's *Paragone*," *Art Bulletin*, XLV, September 1963, pp. 266-71.

Piron, E. A. *Eugène Delacroix: sa vie et ses œuvres*. Paris, Jules Claye, 1865.

Roger-Marx, Claude. "Le plus grand des critiques d'art," *Delacroix*. René Huyghe *et al*. Paris, Hachette, 1963, pp. 205-24.

Rudrauf, Lucien. *Eugène Delacroix et le problème du romantisme artistique*. Paris, Henri Laurens, 1942.

———. "De la bête à l'ange: les étapes de la lutte vitale dans la pensée et l'art d'Eugène Delacroix," *Acta Historiae Artium*, IX, fascicules 3-4, 1963, pp. 295-341.

Sérullaz, Maurice. *Eugène Delacroix: dessins, aquarelles et lavis*. Paris, Editions Albert Morance, 1952.

———. *Les peintures murales de Delacroix*. Paris, Les éditions du temps, 1963.

Sieber-Meier, Christine. *Untersuchungen zum "Œuvre littéraire" von Eugène Delacroix*. Bern, Francke, 1963.

Signac, Paul. *D'Eugène Delacroix au néo-impressionisme*. Paris, Librairie Floury, 1939.

Tourneux, Maurice. *Eugène Delacroix devant ses contemporains*. Paris, Jules Rouam, 1886.

BIBLIOGRAPHY

Venturi, Lionello. "Delacroix," *L'Arte*, new series, II, 1931, pp. 49-76.

Addison, Joseph and Richard Steele. *The Spectator*, ed. G. Gregory Smith. 4 vols. New York, E. P. Dutton & Co., 1909.

Alberti, Leon Battista. *On Painting*, tr. John R. Spencer. New Haven, Yale University Press, 1956.

Aristotle. *The Poetics of Aristotle*, ed. and tr. S. H. Butcher. London, Macmillan and Co., Ltd., 1922.

Bacon, Francis. "Of Beauty," *Bacon's Essays*, ed. R. Whately. London, Parker, 1856.

Baudelaire, Charles. *Curiosités esthétiques, L'Art romantique et autres œuvres critiques de Baudelaire*, ed. Henri Lemaitre. Paris, Garnier frères, 1962.
>
> "Exposition universelle de 1855"
> "L'Œuvre et la vie d'Eugène Delacroix"
> "Salon de 1846"
> "Salon de 1859"

Bellori, Giovanni Pietro. *Vite dei pittori, scultori, ed architetti moderni*. Pisa, Niccolò Capurro, 1821.

Beyle, Marie Henri (Stendhal). "Racine et Shakespeare," *Œuvres complètes de Stendhal*. 2 vols. Paris, Champion, 1925.

Boileau Despréaux, Nicolas. *Œuvres complètes de Boileau Despréaux*. Paris, chez Lefèvre, 1835.
>
> "L'Art poétique"
> "Préface pour l'édition de 1701"
> "Réflexions critiques sur quelques passages du rhéteur Longin"
> "Traité du sublime: ou du merveilleux dans le discours traduit du grec de Longin"

Bottari, Giovanni and Stefano Ticozzi. *Recueil de lettres sur la peinture, la sculpture et l'architecture*, tr. and ed. L.-J. Jay. Paris, Galerie de tableaux, 1817.

Bouhours, Dominique. *Les entretiens d'Ariste et d'Eugène*. Paris, Mabre-Cramoisy, 1671.

Bret, M. "Supplément à la vie de Molière," *Œuvres de Molière*, ed. M. Bret. 6 vols. Paris, Compagnie des libraires associés, 1804.

BIBLIOGRAPHY

Bulgari, Stamati. *Sur le but moral des arts.* Paris, 1827.

Burke, Edmund. *A Philosophical Enquiry into the Origin of Our Ideas of the Sublime and Beautiful.* London, 1812.

Castelvetro, Lodovico. *Poetica d'Aristotele vulgarizzata et sposta.* Basilea, Pietro de Sedabonis, 1576.

Caylus, Comte de. "Discours du Comte de Caylus sur les dessins," *Revue universelle des arts,* IX, 1859, pp. 314-23.

Cennini, Cennino. *The Book of the Art of Cennino Cennini,* tr. C. J. Herringham. London, G. Allen, 1899.

Chateaubriand, François Auguste René. "Génie du Christianisme," *Œuvres de M. le vicomte de Chateaubriand.* 20 vols. Paris, chez Lefèvre, 1833.

Dezallier d'Argenville, A. J. *Abrégé de la vie des plus fameux peintres.* Paris, chez DeBuve, l'ainé, 1744.

Diderot, Denis. *Correspondance,* ed. Georges Roth. Paris, Editions de minuit, 1955.

————. *Diderot Salons,* ed. J. Seznec and J. Adhémar. 2 vols. Oxford, The Clarendon Press, 1957.

————. *Essais sur la peinture,* ed. Roland Desné. Paris, Editions sociales, 1955.

————. "Pensées détachées," *Essais sur la peinture,* pp. 120-99.

————. *Œuvres complètes de Diderot,* ed. J. Assézat. 20 vols. Paris, Garnier frères, 1876.

    "Lettre sur les sourds et muets"

    "Paradoxe sur le comédien"

    "Salon de 1761"

    "Salon de 1763"

    "Salon de 1765"

    "Salon de 1767"

Dolce, Lodovico. *Dialogo della pittura intitolato L'Aretino.* Florence, Michele Nestenus and Francesco Moücke, 1735.

Dubos, Jean Baptiste. *Réflexions critiques sur la poésie et sur la peinture.* 2 vols. Paris, chez Jean Mariette, 1719.

Du Fresnoy, C. A. *L'Art de peinture,* tr. Roger de Piles. Paris, chez C. A. Jombert, 1751.

Dupuy du Grez, Bernard. *Traité sur la peinture pour en apprendre la téorie et se perfectionner dans la pratique.* Toulouse, chez la veuve de J. Pech et A. Pech, 1699.

BIBLIOGRAPHY

Félibien, André. *Conférences de l'académie royale de peinture.* London, chez D. Mortier, 1705.

―――. *Des principes de l'architecture, de la sculpture, de la peinture.* Paris, chez la veuve et J. B. Coignard, fils, 1697.

―――. *Entretiens sur les vies et sur les ouvrages des plus excellens peintres.* 2 vols. 2d ed. Paris, S. Mabre-Cramoisy, 1685-88.

―――. *Entretiens sur la vie et les ouvrages de Nicolas Poussin.* Geneva, P. Cailler, 1947.

Filmer, Edward. *A Defence of Dramatick Poetry.* London, 1698.

Harris, James. "A Discourse on Music, Painting, and Poetry," *Miscellanies by James Harris.* 5 vols. London, 1775-92.

Hogarth, William. *The Analysis of Beauty,* ed. Joseph Burke. Oxford, The Clarendon Press, 1955.

Hugo, Victor. "Victor Hugo raconté par un témoin de sa vie," *Œuvres complètes de Victor Hugo.* 48 vols. Paris, J. Hetzel et Cie.; A. Quantin, 1880-89.

Ingres, Jean Auguste Dominique. *Ecrits sur l'art.* Preface by R. Cogniat. Paris, La jeune parque, 1947.

Kandinsky, W. *Concerning the Spiritual in Art.* New York, Wittenborn, Schultz, Inc., 1947.

Kant, Immanuel. *The Critique of Judgment,* tr. J. H. Bernard. 2d ed. London, Macmillan and Co., 1914.

La Fontaine, Jean de. *Œuvres,* ed. H. Regnier. Paris, Hachette, 1883-97.

La Rochefoucauld, François de. *Œuvres complètes,* ed. L. Martin-Chauffier. Argenteuil, H. Barthélemy, 1935.

―――. "Réflexions diverses," *Œuvres de la Rochefoucauld.* 3 vols. Paris, Hachette, 1868.

Lessing, Gotthold Ephraim. *Laocoon,* tr. E. Frothingham. New York, The Noonday Press, 1957.

Lomazzo, Giovanni Paolo. *A Tracte Containing the Artes of Curious Paintings,* tr. R. Haydock. Oxford, J. Barnes, 1598.

―――. *Trattato dell'arte della pittura, scultura, ed architettura.* 3 vols. Rome, Del-Monte, 1844.

Longinus, Cassius. *On the Sublime,* tr. W. H. Fyfe. London, W. Heinemann, Ltd., 1927.

Mascardi, Agostino. *Dell'arte historica.* Rome, appresso G. Facciotti, 1636.

BIBLIOGRAPHY

Medwin, Thomas. *The Journal of the Conversations of Lord Byron.* New York, Wilder and Campbell, 1824.

Montesquieu, Charles Louis de Secondat. *Œuvres complètes de Montesquieu.* 7 vols. Paris, Garnery, 1823.
"Essai sur le goût dans les choses de la nature et de l'art"
"Pensées diverses"

Mozart, Wolfgang Amadeus, *et al. The Letters of Mozart and his Family,* tr. and ed. E. Anderson. London, Macmillan and Co., Ltd., 1938.

Perrault, Charles. *Parallèles des anciens et des modernes en ce qui regarde les arts et les sciences.* 4 vols. 2d ed. Paris, Coignard, 1692-96.

Piles, Roger de. *Abrégé de la vie des peintres.* Paris, chez François Muguet, 1699.

⸻. "Conversations sur la peinture," *Recueil de divers ouvrages sur la peinture et le coloris.* Paris, chez C. A. Jombert, 1755.

⸻. *Cours de peinture par principes.* Paris, chez Jacques Estienne, 1708.

⸻. *Dialogue sur le coloris.* Paris, chez N. Langlois, 1699.

⸻. "Dissertation sur les ouvrages des plus fameux peintres," *Recueil de divers ouvrages sur la peinture et le coloris.* Paris, chez C. A. Jombert, 1755.

Planet, Louis de. *Souvenirs de travaux de peinture avec M. Eugène Delacroix,* ed. A. Joubin. Paris, Librairie Armand Colin, 1929.

Plinius Secundus, C. *The Elder Pliny's Chapters on the History of Art,* tr. K. Jex-Blake and ed. E. Sellers. London, Macmillan and Co., 1896.

Plotinus. *The Ethical Treatises,* tr. S. MacKenna. London, Philip Lee Warner, 1917.

Plutarch. "How the Young Man Should Study Poetry," *Moralia,* tr. F. C. Babbitt. London, W. Heinemann, Ltd., 1927.

Poe, Edgar Allan. *Histoires extraordinaires,* tr. C. Baudelaire. Paris, Levy, 1875.

Poussin, Nicolas. *Lettres de Poussin,* ed. Pierre du Colombier. Paris, Cité des livres, 1929.

⸻. *Collection de lettres de Nicolas Poussin,* ed. Quatremère de Quincy. Paris, 1824.

⸻. "Observations on Painting," in Elizabeth Holt (ed.),

Literary Sources of Art History. Princeton, Princeton University Press, 1947, pp. 366-69.

Quatremère de Quincy. *Essai sur l'idéal dans ses applications pratiques aux œuvres de l'imitation propre des arts du dessin*. Paris, Librairie d'Adrien le Clère et Cie., 1837.

Rapin, René. "Réflexions sur la poétique," *Œuvres*. 2 vols. The Hague, chez Pierre Gosse, 1725.

Rousseau, Jean-Jacques. *Les Confessions*. Paris, Georges Crès et Cie., 1912.

———. *Œuvres complètes de J. J. Rousseau*. 17 vols. Paris, Armand-Aubrée, 1830-33.

    "Correspondance"

    "Essai sur l'origine de langues"

Rubens, Peter Paul. *De imitatione antiquarum statuarum*, tr. Roger de Piles in *Cours de peinture par principes*, pp. 139-48.

Sand, George. "Impressions et souvenirs," *Œuvres complètes de George Sand*. 55 vols. Paris, Michel Levy, 1865-97.

Schiller, Johann Christoph Friedrich von. "Upon the Aesthetic Culture of Man, in a Series of Letters," *The Philosophical and Aesthetic Letters and Essays of Schiller*, tr. J. Weiss. London, John Chapman, 1845.

Schlegel, August Wilhelm von. *Lectures on Dramatic Art and Literature*, tr. John Black. 2d ed. London, George Bell and Sons, 1894.

Senancour, Etienne Pivert de. *Oberman*: *Lettres publiées par M. . . . Senancour*. 3 vols. Grenoble, B. Arthaud, 1947.

Staël, Madame de. *De l'Allemagne*. Paris, Charpentier, 1869.

Varchi, B. *Due lezioni sopra la pittura e scultura*. Florence, L. Torrentino, 1549.

Vinci, Leonardo da. *Paragone*: *A Comparison of the Arts*, tr. Irma A. Richter. New York, Oxford University Press, 1949.

———. *Traité de la peinture de Léonard de Vinci*, tr. Roland Fréart Sieur de Chambray. Paris, Langlois, 1651.

———. *Traité de la peinture par Léonard de Vinci*, tr. Pierre François Giffart. Paris, 1716.

———. *Traité de la peinture de Léonard de Vinci*, tr. P. M. Gault de St. Germain. Paris, Perlet, 1803.

————. *Treatise on Painting*, tr. A. Philip McMahon. 2 vols. Princeton, Princeton University Press, 1956.

Voltaire, François Marie Arouet de. *Œuvres complètes de Voltaire*. 97 vols. Paris, Delangle frères, 1826-34.
    "Discours sur la tragédie"
    "Mélanges littéraires"

————. *Questions sur l'Encyclopédie par des amateurs*. 3 vols. Geneva, 1771.

Wackenroder, Wilhelm Heinrich. "Phantasien über die Kunst für Freunde der Kunst," *Werke und Briefe*. 2 vols. Jena, Diederichs, 1910.

Wark, Robert R. (ed.). *Sir Joshua Reynolds: Discourses on Art*. San Marino, Huntington Library, 1959.

Winckelmann, Johann J. "Thoughts on the Imitation of Greek Art in Painting and Sculpture." *Literary Sources of Art History*, ed. Elizabeth Holt. Princeton, Princeton University Press, 1947, pp. 522-34.

Wordsworth, William. "The Prelude," *The Complete Poetical Works of William Wordsworth*. 10 vols. Boston, Houghton Mifflin Co., 1910.

Young, Edward. "Conjectures on Original Composition," *The Works of the Author of the Night-Thoughts*. 5 vols. London, 1767-73.

BOOKS AND MONOGRAPHS

Abrams, M. H. *The Mirror and the Lamp: Romantic Theory and the Critical Tradition*. New York, Oxford University Press, 1953.

Addison, Agnes. *Romanticism and the Gothic Revival*. New York, Richard R. Smith, 1938.

Babbitt, Irving. *Rousseau and Romanticism*. New York, Meridian Books, 1955.

Bate, Walter Jackson. *From Classic to Romantic: Premises of Taste in Eighteenth Century England*. New York, Harper and Brothers, 1961.

Borgerhoff, E. B. O. *The Freedom of French Classicism*. Princeton, Princeton University Press, 1950.

Butcher, S. H. *Aristotle's Theory of Poetry and Fine Art*. London, Macmillan and Co., Ltd., 1895.

BIBLIOGRAPHY

Chambers, F. P. *The History of Taste*. New York, Columbia University Press, 1932.

Charlton, H. B. *Castelvetro's Theory of Poetry*. Manchester, Manchester University Press, 1913.

Clark, Kenneth. *The Gothic Revival*. London, Constable and Co., Ltd., 1928.

Clements, Robert J. *Michelangelo's Theory of Art*. New York, New York University Press, 1961.

Delécluze, Etienne J. *Louis David: son école et son temps*. Paris, Didier, 1855.

Du Camp, Maxime. *Souvenirs littéraires de Maxime du Camp: 1822-1894*. Introduction by Henri Lemaitre. Paris, Hachette, 1962.

Estève, Edmond. *Byron et le romantisme français*. Paris, Hachette, 1907.

Fergusson, Francis. *The Idea of a Theater*. Princeton, Princeton University Press, 1949.

Folkierski, W. *Entre le classicisme et le romantisme*. Cracovie, Académie polonaise des sciences et des lettres, 1925.

Fontaine, André. *Les doctrines d'art en France*. Paris, Librairie Renouard-H. Laurens, 1909.

Friedlaender, Walter F. *David to Delacroix*, tr. Robert Goldwater. Cambridge, Harvard University Press, 1952.

Frankl, Paul. *The Gothic: Literary Sources and Interpretations through Eight Centuries*. Princeton, Princeton University Press, 1960.

Gautier, Théophile. *Histoire du romantisme suivi de notices romantiques et d'une étude sur la poésie française: 1830-68*. Paris, Bibliothèque Charpentier, 1895.

Gilbert, Katherine and Helmut Kuhn. *A History of Esthetics*. New York, The Macmillan Co., 1939.

Gilman, Margaret. *Baudelaire the Critic*. New York, Columbia University Press, 1943.

Goldwater, Robert and Marco Treves. *Artists on Art*. New York, Pantheon, 1945.

Green, Frederick C. *Jean-Jacques Rousseau: A Critical Study of his Life and Writings*. Cambridge, Cambridge University Press, 1955.

BIBLIOGRAPHY

Herbert, Robert L. *Barbizon Revisited*. New York, Clarke and Way, 1962.

Holt, Elizabeth. *Literary Sources of Art History*. Princeton, Princeton University Press, 1947.

Horner, Lucie. *Baudelaire: critique de Delacroix*. Geneva, Librairie E. Droz, 1956.

Jamot, Paul, *et al. Le romantisme et l'art*. Paris, 1928.

Lasserre, Pierre. *Le romantisme français*. Paris, Société du "Mercure de France," 1907.

Marçais, Georges. *Le costume musulman d'Alger*. Paris, Plon, 1930.

May, Gita. *Diderot et Baudelaire: critiques d'art*. Geneva, Librairie E. Droz, 1957.

Monk, Samuel H. *The Sublime: A Study of Critical Theories in XVIII Century England*. New York, Modern Language Association of America, 1935.

Panofsky, Erwin. *Idea: ein Beitrag zur Begriffsgeschichte der älteren Kunsttheorie*. Berlin, Verlag Bruno Hessling, 1960.

Pepper, Stephen C. *World Hypotheses*. Berkeley, University of California Press, 1942.

Praz, Mario. *The Romantic Agony*. New York, Meridian Books, 1956.

Rookmaker, H. R. *Synthetist Art Theories*. Amsterdam, Swets, 1959.

Rooses, Max. *L'Œuvre de P. P. Rubens*. 5 vols. Antwerp, J. Maes, 1886-92.

Rosenthal, Léon. *Du romantisme au réalisme*. Paris, Librairie Renouard, 1914.

———. *La peinture romantique*. Paris, L.-Henry May, 1900.

Saintsbury, George. *A History of Criticism and Literary Taste in Europe*. London, William Blackwood and Sons, 1902.

Schlosser-Magnino, Julius. *La letteratura artistica*. Florence, "La nuova Italia," 1935.

Seltman, Charles. *Greek Coins*. London, Methuen, 1933.

Sloane, Joseph C. *Paul Marc Joseph Chenavard: Artist of 1848*. Chapel Hill, The University of North Carolina Press, 1962.

Spingarn, J. E. *A History of Literary Criticism in the Renaissance*. 2d ed. New York, Columbia University Press, 1924.

BIBLIOGRAPHY

Vallois, M. *La formation de l'influence Kantienne en France.* Paris, Librairie Félix Alcan, n.d.

ARTICLES

Blunt, Anthony. "Poussin's Notes on Painting," *Journal of the Warburg Institute*, I, April 1938, pp. 344-51.

Clément, M. "Léonard de Vinci," *Revue des Deux-Mondes*, XXVI, April 1860, pp. 603-43.

Clements, Robert J. "Michelangelo on Effort and Rapidity in Art," *Journal of the Warburg and Courtauld Institutes*, XVII, 1954, pp. 301-10.

Egbert, Donald D. "Organic Expression and Architecture," *Evolutionary Thought in America*, ed. S. Persons. New Haven, 1950, pp. 336-96.

Gide, André. "Réponse à une enquête de 'La Renaissance' sur le classicisme." *Œuvres complètes d'André Gide*, ed. L. Martin-Chauffier. Paris, Nouvelle revue française, 1932-39.

Gilman, Margaret. "Imagination and Creation in Diderot," *Diderot Studies*. 2 vols. Syracuse, Syracuse University Press, 1949-52, II, pp. 200-20.

———. "The Poet According to Diderot," *Romanic Review*, XXXVII, February 1946, pp. 34-54.

Kristeller, Paul O. "The Modern System of the Arts: A Study of the History of Aesthetics," *Journal of the History of Ideas*, XII, 1951, pp. 496-527; and *ibid.*, XIII, 1952, pp. 17-46.

Lee, Rensselaer W. Review of *Artistic Theory in Italy: 1450-1600* by Anthony Blunt, *Art Bulletin*, XXIII, December 1941, pp. 332-35.

———. "*Ut Pictura Poesis*: The Humanistic Theory of Painting," *Art Bulletin*, XXII, December 1940, pp. 197-269.

Lovejoy, Arthur O. "On the Discrimination of Romanticisms," *PMLA*, XXXIX, 1924, pp. 229-53.

———. "Schiller and the Genesis of German Romanticism," *Modern Language Notes*, XXXV, January 1920, pp. 1-10; and *ibid.*, March 1920, pp. 136-46.

———. "The First Gothic Revival and the Return to Nature," *Modern Language Notes*, XXVII, 1932, pp. 414-46.

BIBLIOGRAPHY

Monk, Samuel H. "A Grace Beyond the Reach of Art," *Journal of the History of Ideas*, v, April 1944, pp. 131-50.

Scudo, S. "Wolfgang Mozart et l'opéra de Don Juan," *Revue des Deux-Mondes*, I, March 1849, pp. 872-925.

Vitet, L. "Pindare et l'art grec," *Revue des Deux-Mondes*, xxv, February 1860, pp. 711-26.

INDEX

Entries under Eugène Delacroix relate to major aspects of his theory and to his writings and paintings. Significant paintings by other artists are entered separately, followed by the artist's name in parentheses. Authors who provide important sources for Delacroix's thought or who can be related to his thought are entered separately with citation of their works. For supplementary aspects of Delacroix's theory and their sources, see separate entries under such topics as counterpoint, reflections, subjectivity, etc.

INDEX

INDEX

INDEX

INDEX